EVERGLADES

EVERGLADES

An Ecosystem Facing Choices and Challenges

Anne Ake

Pineapple Press, Inc.
Sarasota, Florida

This book is for
Dooge, my mother
One of the great ladies of the South
and
Tyler, my grandson
The light of my life
At five and eighty-five they share the ability to view the
world with a blend of wisdom, humor, and awe.

Inquiries should be addressed to:

Pineapple Press, Inc.
P.O. Box 3889
Sarasota, Florida 34230

www.pineapplepress.com

Library of Congress Cataloging-in-Publication Data

Ake, Anne
  Everglades : an ecosystem facing choices and challenges / Anne Ake. -- 1st ed.
      p. cm.
  Includes bibliographical references and index.
  ISBN 978-1-56164-410-0 (hardback : alk. paper)
  1. Everglades (Fla.)--Environmental conditions--Juvenile literature. 2. Wetland ecology--Florida--Everglades--Juvenile literature.
3. Natural history--Florida--Everglades--Juvenile literature. 4. Environmental protection--Florida--Everglades--Juvenile literature.
I. Title.
  QH105.F6A44 2007
  577.6809759'39--dc22

                                                    2007040418

First Edition
10 9 8 7 6 5 4 3 2 1

Design by Anne Ake. Layout by Shé Heaton
Printed in the United States of America

Contents

Acknowledgments

This book is a tribute to my husband Bill, a potter, an outdoorsman, a much-loved husband, father, and grandfather. He was always there for me with good ideas, photos, and criticism. Most of all, he made doing the book fun. He did not live to see the finished product.

Many people have helped to see this book from concept to press. My heartfelt thank you goes to each of you. A very special thank you goes to biologist and endangered species specialist Larry Ogren, who has shared his expertise, good talk, and friendship from start to finish. Dr. Jeffery Schmid and Jill Schmid contributed valuable information and two great days of exploring and photographing. Biologists Dr. Ed Keppner and Lisa Keppner not only did an excellent critique, but a top-notch proofing job. Jackie and Walt Frazer helped chase down elusive facts and opened their home to us. I thank Jeannette Hobbs, Sherrie Kreth, Jim Arendale, Ginny Svoboda, Paul Gray, James Newman, the Bonita Bay Group, the Marshall Foundation, the Conservancy of Southwest Florida, and State Archives of Florida for the generous loan of photographs.

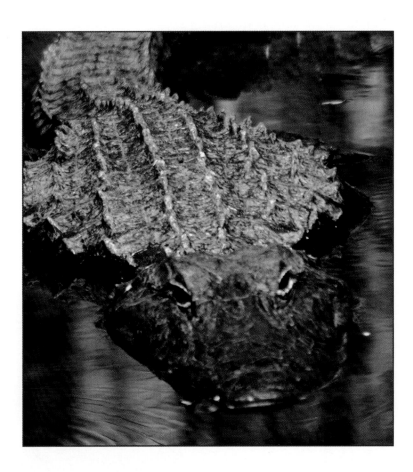

Introduction

Napoleon Bonaparte Broward, then governor of Florida, called it a "pestilence-ridden swamp." He hated it and wanted to fix it—make it useful. Marjory Stoneman Douglas called it the "River of Grass." She loved it and devoted most of her 108 years to preserving its wild beauty. Broward and others dammed, diked, ditched, and drained thousands of acres. Douglas and her followers fought to save the ecosystem from developers, farmers, and Florida politics. Today, the focus of their passion, the Florida Everglades, is sometimes called the "end of the pipe"—and the pipe is draining the lifeblood of an ecosystem unlike any other in the world. The Everglades is vast and beautiful, but it is wounded, perhaps bleeding out faster than last-minute first aid can control.

The rains that fall on south Florida in the spring and summer join with the overflow from Lake Okeechobee to create the Everglades, a great wetland unlike any other on earth. Since humans first arrived in this wilderness they have gobbled up its resources as if they were endless. And, indeed, it would have appeared that way. In the beginning, the Everglades covered the entire southern third of Florida. Life was everywhere—alligators, crocodiles, panthers, deer, and birds in such numbers that passing flocks often darkened the sky. But the ecosystem was a delicately balanced mechanism and human intervention has upset that balance. The Everglades has suffered from over-development, large-scale agriculture, political favoritism, and from well-intentioned attempts to second-guess Mother Nature.

The Everglades was named a World Heritage Site and an International Biosphere Reserve by UNESCO, and designated a Wetland of International Importance by the Ramsar Convention on Wetlands. In spite of recognition of its global significance, the ecosystem continues to decline. The latest attempt to preserve the Everglades, the Comprehensive Everglades Restoration Plan (CERP), is being tugged this way and that by developers, farmers, and politicians. The issues are complex.

It is all about the water. South Florida residents, tourists, farmers, industrialists, and developers all have legitimate water needs. They want just the right amount of water where and when they need it. Where there is too much water, they want it pushed out of the way and put somewhere more convenient. So the natural flow of the water has been manipulated to provide for everyone's needs. The needs of the Everglades were ignored or not understood and the effect has been devastating.

The point to remember is that the Everglades provides the water. So the human population is dependent on a healthy Everglades for an adequate water supply. William Ruckelshaus, the first EPA Administrator, said, "Nature provides a free lunch, but only if we control our appetites." This book is about the beauty and value of the Everglades and about learning to make sacrifices in order to maintain a healthy planet.

EVERGLADES

Chapter 1
Everglades
Exploring a Unique Ecosystem

There are no other Everglades in the world. They are, they have always been,
one of the unique regions of the earth; remote, never wholly known.
Nothing anywhere else is like them ... —Marjory Stoneman Douglas

The Everglades includes varied habitats, but sawgrass prairie dotted with tree islands is the heart
of the Everglades. The vast vistas of waving sawgrass inspired Marjory Stoneman Douglas to call the
Everglades the "River of Grass."

he heart of the Everglades is a great river that slides almost imperceptibly across south Florida. It does not look like a river. It is too wide. At some points, it stretches fifty miles from shore to shore. It does not carry riverboats loaded with goods and passengers. It is too shallow—about three feet in the depths of the channels and only six inches deep across much of its width. It does not slice through mountains or pound boulders into sand in its rush to reach the sea. Instead, it slips serenely across the land at a rate of 100 feet (30 meters) per day. It looks more like a marsh than a river, because it is filled with waving aquatic grasses. Yet it is a river—and a mighty one—because it drives a huge ecosystem.

Conservationist Marjory Stoneman Douglas called it the "River of Grass." River of grass is a beautiful description of the thousands of acres of aquatic grass and sedge washed by the gently flowing water, but it is not a complete picture. The Everglades is not all marsh. It is a complex ecosystem adapted to the flow of the water.

The word ecosystem refers to the web of connections between organisms and their physical environment. An ecosystem may contain a variety of habitats. An area of higher ground, for example, may be a habitat for a mouse that can't live on constantly wet ground, while marsh provides other organisms just what they need. But both habitats are part of a larger ecosystem.

The Everglades ecosystem ends with the sea but the beginning point is not as distinct. Estimates of the size of the Everglades vary because people define the Everglades in different ways. Many people think of the Everglades as the remaining wilderness lands, and others narrow the definition further to mean the land protected by the Everglades National Park. Locals often colloquially refer to the wild Everglades simply as the Glades. However, the Everglades ecosystem originally comprised the entire southern third of Florida. Today, the highly developed coastal areas of southern

I Live in the Glades

Anoles

The green anole (*Anolis carolinensis*) is often mistakenly called a Florida chameleon because it can change colors from bright green to shades of brown and, when stressed or injured, almost black. The green anole is not as common in the Everglades as it once was because of competition for food and habitat from the brown or Cuban anole (*Anolis sagrei*), an exotic species that is spreading rapidly in south Florida. The two look very much alike when the green anole is in its brown coloration, but the brown anole cannot turn green.

Florida are still dependent on maintaining a healthy Everglades ecosystem.

Why are there Everglades?

When most of the earth's land masses were firmly established, Florida was still undecided as to whether it would be land or sea. The low-lying land changed size and shape with the whims of the sea. Each time the sea claimed the land as its own it brought a load of calcium and a horde of bryozoans—tiny creatures with calcium shells. The sea calcium formed grains called ooids and dropped to the bottom. The bryozoans died and joined the ooids. Eventually they bonded together to become limestone.

The limestone built into a mass of jagged crags and holes. It rose up into low ridges around the edges of what is now south Florida and flattened into a shallow basin in the middle. The limestone was porous and water flowed through it and over it. The sea slipped away one last time and left the Florida peninsula barely above sea level. Plants began to grow and animals from the Caribbean to the south and from farther north on the continent moved in. An unusual blend of tropical and temperate plants and animals populated the peninsula. Roots and other plant matter gradually formed a thick mat of peat. The peat soil was dense and black, and its low oxygen content made it resistant to decay.

Most of the year a layer of water still washed over the peat, and underneath it water flowed through the limestone to form the Biscayne Aquifer. This aquifer that lies just beneath the surface provides the fresh water for south Florida. This geologic design resembling a water-filled saucer set the stage for the development of a unique ecosystem—the Everglades.

Where it all starts

The Everglades ecosystem starts near Orlando. It carries runoff rainwater from central Florida southward until it evaporates and falls again as rain, seeps into the ground to return to the aquifer, or runs into the sea to nourish the estuaries. Thus, the cycle of life in the Everglades begins with the central Florida rain. Beginning in May, the storms build and drenching rain washes over the land. By October 40 to 65 inches (100 to 165 cm) may fall. Some of it gathers in puddles, and the puddles run together to form pools, the pools overflow to form small creeks and watery prairies that flow into lakes. The lakes overflow into bigger creeks that flow into the Kissimmee River and continue southward to Lake Okeechobee.

Okeechobee is a Seminole word meaning "big water," and the lake of that name is the largest body of fresh water south of the Great Lakes. It stretches 37 miles (60 km) long by 30 miles (48 km) wide. It covers 730 square miles (1891 square kilometers), but it is a shallow lake with an average depth of only 12 feet (3.6 m). The land fed by the flow of water from the lake is the Everglades.

Before humans began diverting much of the water from Lake Okeechobee to

Freshwater sloughs are slightly deeper than the surrounding prairie. The change in depth supports different plant and animal life. This white egret fishes the edge of the slough looking for small fish and invertebrates.

I Live in the Glades

Anhinga

Sometimes people call the anhinga (*Anhinga anhinga*) "snakebird" because it often swims with only its long, thin head and neck out of the water. The anhinga is well adapted to underwater fishing. The eighth and ninth vertebrae in its long neck form a hinge that helps in the quick capture of prey. In addition, unlike most water birds, it does not have oil glands for waterproofing its feathers. The lack of oil makes it less buoyant and enhances its ability to dive and swim. Anhingas are often seen with their wings spread out to dry in the sun.

The male has an all-black body with silver markings on its wings; the female has a brown head and neck.

other uses, it sloshed over the southern banks of the lake to continue its trek to the sea. In the wet season the flat plain became a wide, grassy sheet of water flowing toward the sea. In the dry winter months, much of it turned to dry grassland.

There are other vast wetlands on the planet, but they are fed and drained by a network of rivers and creeks. The Everglades is unique because its water comes from rainfall. Other large wetlands, such as the Pantanal of South America, get most of their water and nutrients from river flooding.

At first glance, the water-driven Everglades ecosystem appears bland and changeless. However, slight variations in elevation, salinity, and soil create a number of distinct habitats within and around the marshy river.

Freshwater sloughs

The first image that comes to mind when most people think of the Everglades is the wet inland habitat. That habitat includes the sloughs—the main channels of the river. This is where the water speeds along at a pace of 100 feet (30 meters)—one-third the length of a football field per day. The sloughs move from north to south through a thick growth of sawgrass. Two distinct sloughs run through Everglades National Park: Shark River Slough, the central waterway of the "River of Grass"; and to its east, narrow Taylor Slough. Other sloughs run through Big Cypress Swamp on the western edge of the remaining Everglades wilderness. In the center of the sloughs, where the water is more permanent and deeper, the vegetation changes—water lilies and other broadleaf marsh plants replace the sawgrass.

Is it a Prairie or a Marsh?

Much of the Everglades is prairie or marsh. Prairies and marshes are different, but they often blend into each other or exist next to each other. Praries and marshes, like other wetland habitats, are classified by their hydroperiods, or the number of months per year they are typically covered with water.

Wet prairie is the predominant habitat of the Everglades. Wet prairies are flooded, or at least soggy, for two to five months of the year. Sawgrass and other grasses, sedges, and rushes grow here, and a variety of wildflowers break the monotony. Frogs, salamanders, snakes, snails, insects, spiders, and birds feed or live in the wet prairies.

Dry prairies seldom flood and support plants such as saw palmetto, wiregrass, and other grasses. They are subject to frequent lightning fires. Like wet prairies, they boast many wildflowers, but of different varieties.

Freshwater marshes are similar to wet prairies, but are wetter. They stay wet for six to nine months of the year. Some marshes are just small areas bordering alligator holes, ponds, or canals. They support different types of plants, including cattails and broadleaf plants such as arrowroot, fireflag, and pickerelweed. Many birds nest here, raccoons hunt food, and otters build dens in the soft banks.

Salt marshes form a transitional zone between the mangroves and freshwater wetlands. Salt marsh plants include a variety of grasses and Christmas berry, but often wet prairie plants mingle with them. Wading birds like to feed here, and bobcats hunt rabbits and rats.

I Live in the Glades

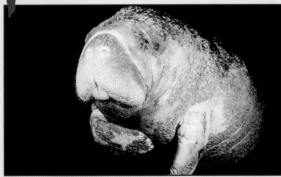

Manatee

The endangered West Indian manatee (*Trichecus manatus*) spends winters in south Florida, but sometimes travels to other areas in the warm summer months. Manatees are large, gentle, slow-moving aquatic mammals distantly related to the elephant. The average adult is 10 to 12 feet long (3 to 3.5 meters) and weighs 800 to 1200 pounds (362 to 544 kg), but they have been known to grow as large as 13 feet (3.9 meters) and 3500 pounds (1587 kg).

Manatees feed on a variety of aquatic plants and can eat 10 to 15 percent of their body weight a day. They use their large flexible lip much as an elephant uses its trunk to grab food and put it in their mouths. Manatees are highly tolerant to changes in salinity and can be found in rivers, estuaries, saltwater bays, canals, and coastal areas.

Researchers estimate that there are fewer than 3,000 West Indian manatees remaining. They have no natural enemies except humans and their machines. Many manatees are killed or wounded by boat propellers, crushed or drowned by locks, or die from eating hooks, monofilament line, or other debris. Boat propellers are such a hazard to manatees that researchers often use the pattern of propeller scars on their body as a way to tell one from another.

Freshwater prairie

Shallow freshwater prairie borders the sloughs. Prairie in Florida has a different meaning from the dry grasslands of the midwestern United States. The wet prairies of the Everglades look a lot like the sloughs, but they are only inches deep as opposed to the sloughs, which are two to three feet deep. The prairies support a thick growth of sawgrass, which gradually gives way to the plants that grow in the deeper water of the sloughs. The borders of the changing habitat are indistinct and the whole area has a marshy look.

Tree islands

Within this watery world, many small tree islands thrust up above the sawgrass of the sloughs and prairie. There are two types of tree islands—hammocks and heads. Heads are groups of wetland trees that grow in depressions in the limestone. Heads are named for the type of tree they support. There are cypress heads, bay heads, and willow heads.

Hammocks are dense growths of hardwood trees and other plants on slightly elevated land. They form one of the most diverse and important habitats in the Everglades. Hammocks in the slough develop a teardrop shape as the erosive power of the sluggish water wears the downstream end to a point. The hammocks in the even slower waters of the prairie tend to be round in shape. The hammocks

Cypress and hardwood swamps are a sharp contrast to the airy open vistas of the sawgrass prairie, but are important Everglades habitat.

hold rich soil and support the growth of hardwood trees. Familiar trees, including live oak, red maple, and hackberry, mingle with tropical species such as mahogany, gumbo-limbo, and cocoplum. Ferns and air plants thrive in the moist shade of the hammocks.

Although they are only slightly higher than the surrounding land, hammocks rarely flood. Hammocks and other tree islands are not often damaged by fire because acids from decaying plants dissolve the limestone around tree islands and create natural moats that protect the plants from fire.

Pinelands

Pinelands consist of slash pine with an understory of saw palmettos and more than 200 varieties of tropical plants. They are the most diverse habitat in the Everglades. The pinelands perch on top of limestone ridges, and the pines send their roots into cracks and crevices where soil collects in the bedrock. Florida naturalist Archie Carr loved the rugged beauty of the pinelands. He describes the struggle faced by the plants there:

"To see what a plant is up against in this region you ought to look at a pine tree that has been pushed over by a bulldozer—at the upturned disk of desperate roots that in their sculpturing reflect every irregularity in the crazy stone surface they had grown on. Nevertheless, some of the pines used to reach heights of 80 or 90 feet."

The pinelands are the driest part of the Everglades and fire often sweeps through them. The fire insures their continued existence. Fire clears the faster-growing hardwoods that would rob the pines of nutrients and light. The pines survive the fire because they are insulated by multi-layered bark and only the outer layers are scorched. Other plants of the pinelands have their own adaptations for fire survival. For example, the bulbous roots of the coontie (once a popular food plant of the Indians) allow rapid regrowth after a fire.

Cypress

While the plants of the pinelands and the hammocks grab the few bits of high ground, other trees of the Everglades thrive with their feet in the water.

The cypress tree is a deciduous conifer that can survive in standing water. Some cypresses form large domes in natural soil-filled depressions in the limestone base. The trees grow tall in the center of these depressions and gradually get smaller as the soil gets poorer nearer the edges, creating the distinctive dome shape. Often the domes are donut-shaped when seen from the air, as they enclose ponds of deeper water in the center. Trees in the center of the domes sometimes reach 100 feet (30 m) in height.

Many other plants depend on the cypress trees for a place to grow. The trees provide a perching place for epiphytes such as orchids and bromeliads. These plants that take nourishment from the air are not parasites. They take nothing from the cypress, but simply wrap their roots around them for support. Cypress domes and the surrounding prairies filled with stunted pond cypress are very typical of Big Cypress Swamp on the northern edge of the Everglades. A swamp is a forested wetland. Big Cypress Swamp looks something like a tropical jungle with its trees bedecked with ferns and colorful flowering epiphytes. The Fakahatchee Strand in the western Big Cypress is a narrow forested channel of pop ash and pond apple. A number of orchids are only found here. Until recently biologists believed the Fakahatchee Strand to be the only place the endangered ghost orchid still survived. However, in July 2007, for the first time in 12 years, a ghost orchid was found blooming in Corkscrew Swamp Sanctuary.

Several salt-tolerant habitats

As the River of Grass finally nears the sea, the landscape changes. Several new habitats influenced by the nearness of the salt water appear. The coastal prairie is an arid region bordering the tidal mud flats of Florida Bay. It gets battered by heavy winds and waves thrown up by tropical storms. Only salt-tolerant vegetation, such as succulents and other low-growing plants similar to desert plants, can live in these harsh conditions.

Along the southern shores, fresh water from the Everglades mixes with salt water. Here red mangrove trees stand poised above the tidal waters on bare stiltlike roots. This estuary is a valuable nursery for shrimp and fish. In addition, it provides feeding grounds and shelter for wading birds and other birds that nest in the mangrove branches.

Spanning the gap between prairie and sea, Florida Bay forms an estuarine to marine habitat with more than 850 square

The appearance of young mangroves in the landscape is an indication of the nearness of salt water.

miles (2072 square kilometers) of marine bottom. Seagrass covers much of it. The seagrass stabilizes the bottom sediments and prevents erosion. In addition, it provides breeding grounds for fish and shellfish and sustains the food chain that supports the higher vertebrates in the bay. Corals and sponges make their homes in the hard bottom areas.

As the shoreline curves northward along the Gulf of Mexico, the land breaks into a multitude of small islands resembling scattered crumbs from a bite taken out of the mainland. This area, known as the Ten Thousand Islands, was once a hideout for rebels and outlaws. Today it is a popular recreational area and provides breeding grounds for fish and crustaceans.

This is the Everglades, ideally. But time and man have wrought changes in the ecosystem—changes so severe that in spite of restoration efforts the survival of the Everglades is in doubt.

What is happening to the Everglades?

Historically, the waters came on cue in the spring and summer. When the rains stopped, the land dried out, and lightning storms brought fire. It worked. The water brought life. The dry season and fires controlled it. The dry season stopped the rampant growth of water-loving plants and kept them from choking the system. The fire cleared underbrush and made room for new seedlings to sprout. The fire also kept some animal populations from growing out of bounds. It all worked together to sustain a stable environment.

Red Mangrove, the First Real Estate Developer

The red mangrove (*Rhizophora mangle*) is an island builder. The name mangrove is used loosely to describe a number of trees that grow in tidal habitat. The red mangrove can be easily spotted standing above the water on a tangle of exposed roots. Its roots catch passing bits of floating leaves, seaweed, and other detritus. The trapped debris decays, drops to the bottom, and forms new soil. The soil gradually builds until it is above water level, and a new island is born. The mangrove also serves as nature's condominium. Fiddler crabs, juvenile fish, and other underwater creatures make their homes in the underwater roots. The hard surfaces of the roots themselves host a variety of algae, sponges, sea squirts, and barnacles, while upstairs in the branches pelicans and other birds raise their families in crowded rookeries.

The mangrove clings tenaciously to shifting ground and tolerates high salt and low oxygen levels. It can spread out horizontally, putting down new roots as it goes, or it can grow from specialized seedlings. Mangrove seeds begin to grow while still attached to the parent tree. By the time the seedlings drop off the tree they are 6 to 12 inches long. They may take root and grow where they fall or they may be carried by the tides for hundreds of miles. Eventually they touch bottom in shallow water and begin to grow. The many islands off the south Florida coast were started by traveling mangroves.

Then humans appeared with their penchant for fixing things. Even the earliest human inhabitants wanted to fix the land—to make it better suit their needs. The Indians saw the effects of natural fires on the rich prairie lands at the northern fringe of the Everglades and began to light fires of their own. The fires flushed out game, killed ticks and poisonous snakes, and cleared land for grazing. Fire was not new to the area, and a few manmade blazes did not cause major changes.

Then white ranchers came to the northern Everglades and set more and bigger fires. Carr writes: " . . . they did the same, only worse, because they were more uneasy than the Indians about snakes, ticks and the black wolves that howled in the night." The

manmade fires and the crops planted on the burned-off land began to change the landscape. As more people moved in, the fires, especially the natural fires, became a menace. Now, fire threatened homes and property, so the people turned their attention to preventing wildfires. At that time, the relationship between fire and life was not understood. No one linked further changes to the nature of the Everglades with the absence of fire.

Besides, the ranchers had other things on their minds. The northern prairies were fertile and productive, but the watering system was messy. The land went dry when plants needed water, and too much water flowed through when drier conditions would be better. Sometimes floods washed

The Ten Thousand Islands were formed by soil-building red mangrove trees. In pioneering days many of these islands were inhabited by farmers or hunters and their families, although there was no source of fresh water except rain.

mangrove snake

Everglades racer

Snakes

There are 26 snake species that occur naturally in Everglades National Park, plus several exotic species that are taking over habitats and crowding native species out. Snakes eat a variety of small creatures, eggs, and sometimes each other. In a healthy environment they play an important role in keeping populations healthy and in appropriate numbers.

The beautiful red-orange of this mangrove snake (*Natrix fasciata compressicauda*) is just one of several color variations. The small mangrove snake, usually between 15 and 30 inches (38 to 76 cm) long, lives in mangroves swamps in or near brackish to salt water. Everglades racers (*Coluber constrictor priapus*) prefer to live in open grasslands or light forest. They are long, thin snakes that can move fast and sometimes climb trees to steal eggs from bird nests.

Two of the four snakes pictured here are venomous. The Florida cottonmouth (*Aghistrodon piscivorus*) lives in or near water. The eastern diamondback rattlesnake (*Crotalus adamanteus*) prefers drier pinelands. Both are large, heavy-bodied snakes that sometimes reach seven feet (two meters) or more.

eastern diamondback rattlesnake

Florida cottonmouth

away crops and homes and threatened lives. So the inhabitants of the Everglades went to work to tidy up and make things better. They straightened meandering streams and confined them to canals. The canals also drained wetlands, leaving dry land exposed for farms and ranches. They took charge of Lake Okeechobee. They built levees to hold back the floodwaters that sometimes surged over the southern banks. They built canals to whisk away excess water and locks to lift or lower boat traffic to meet the changing levels of the lake. The result was a neat and tidy water system. Humans could control it almost as easily as we turn on a faucet to draw a bath.

The effect on the Everglades was devastating. The ebb and flow that had shaped the area for millennia became erratic. The delicate balance was upset. Additionally, the water that once meandered through wetlands, cleansing itself naturally, was dumped raw and poisonous into the lake, and from there into the Glades. The water now came bearing phosphates and nitrates—remnants of fertilizers spread on crops. The water was much too rich for the plants and animals of the Glades. The dissolved nutrients cause lower forms of plants, such as algae, to bloom and choke out slow-growing species. When the blooms die off and sink, the rotting process depletes the water of oxygen, which in turn causes fish to die off.

Sometimes people damage the earth through uncaring greed. More often the damage is done by well-meaning individuals who are trying to make a better life, but without understanding the long-term effects of their actions on the environment. For many years, dedicated environmentalists have fought to protect and restore the Glades. At the same time, farmers, industrialists, and city dwellers have fought equally hard to gain dry land on which to build their homes and businesses and water to grow their crops, run their factories, wash their clothes, and brush their teeth.

Finding a happy medium between the needs of humans and the needs of the earth is never easy. In the case of the Everglades and the growing south Florida population the struggle has been long and often bitter and the successes few. In the final analysis, though, humankind cannot succeed without the benefits of a healthy earth.

Chapter 2

A Tapestry of Life
Relationships That Make It Work

*When one tugs at a single thing in nature, he finds
it attached to the rest of the world.* —John Muir

This turtle seems to be unconcerned about the approaching alligator, and the two tolerate each other well until mealtime. In a flash of movement the gator can catch and crush the turtle for a tasty lunch. Note the second gator in the foreground. Alligators spend much of their time submerged with only their eyes and the tips of their snouts out of the water.

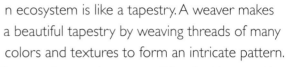 n ecosystem is like a tapestry. A weaver makes a beautiful tapestry by weaving threads of many colors and textures to form an intricate pattern. The weaving creates a new thing that is more than the original spools of thread. But each thread plays a role in the new creation. If some threads are broken or pulled out, the weave becomes looser and the pattern less distinct. If more threads are pulled out, holes appear, and eventually the whole thing falls apart.

Similarly, an ecosystem is woven of all the elements of an environment. The physical features, including geologic features such as soil, water, and elevation, plus atmospheric features such as temperature, humidity, and fire, interweave with the organic features—plants, animals, and microorganisms—to form an intricate pattern of life. All of the parts work together and cannot succeed independently. The physical environment provides nutrients, moisture, and warmth for plants to grow. The plants in turn send their roots into the soil and hold it in place. When they die, they are broken down by microorganisms and become part of the soil. They then provide nutrients for the next generation. Fire keeps it all in check—limiting the growth of aggressive plants and allowing others space to flourish.

Some plants depend on the fire in other ways as well. Several varieties of pine, for example, rely on fire to reproduce. The longleaf pine tree requires a bare uncluttered surface such as burned-off ground to germinate. Its winged seed cannot penetrate a thick layer of duff to reach the soil. South Florida sand pines require heat to sprout. Biologist Larry Ogren says, "There are two types of sand pine in Florida. The southern closed-cone type requires fire to soften resin in the cone and release the seeds. The panhandle type has open cones that do not require heat."

Animals also form an essential part of the weave. They rely on the environment for such things as drinking water and dens to live in. Plants provide them with food, building

I Live in the Glades

material for homes and nests, and cover to hide from predators. Animals help to maintain a healthy balance of species by feeding on plants and other animals. In death, animals feed other animals or return to the earth to maintain the soil's richness. Thus, the elements of an ecosystem create a tightly woven tapestry of life. The threads of the tapestry interact in subtle, often hidden, and almost magical ways. Missing or damaged parts weaken the health of the system.

Alligators—eco-engineers of the Everglades

Some plants or animals play dramatic roles in the ecosystem. The alligator, for example, is one of the most important animals of the Everglades. The alligator is a reptile in a group called crocodilians. There are at least 22 species of crocodilians worldwide, but only two of them are alligators—the American alligator and the Chinese alligator. Two crocodilian species, the American alligator and the American crocodile, are native to North America. Both live in the Ever-

glades—the only place in North America where the American crocodile lives and the only place in the world where crocodiles and alligators live side by side. The American crocodile is rare even in the Everglades. Its range is limited to southern coastal areas; whereas the alligator lives all over the state. The brown caiman, a non-native crocodilian, is occasionally found in the Everglades. Sometimes people buy caimans as pets and later release them into the Everglades.

Unlike the crocodile and the caiman, the American alligator is quite common. It lives in all of Florida as well as other southeastern states, including the Carolinas. Alligators live in swamps, lakes, rivers, and even brackish estuaries and sloughs. They are ideally suited to life in the Everglades.

The word alligator sends chills down the spines of many people. But the American alligator seldom harms humans. Left alone, the alligator goes about the business of being an alligator and in the Glades that makes it a very important citizen.

The way alligators make their living and raise their families is of tremendous impor-

Epiphytes—Tiny Cups of Life

Epiphytes, or air plants, are plants that grow on other living plants. They are not parasites, as they take nothing from the host but a spot in the sun. There are many varieties of epiphytes in the Everglades. The most common epiphytes are orchids and bromeliads. Thousands of these plants festoon the trees of Big Cypress Swamp, adding color and excitement to the landscape.

Bromeliads, most of which are epiphytes, play an important role in the Everglades. The bases of the leaves form cups that hold tiny reservoirs of rainwater, which can last through the dry season. The water helps the bromeliad stay alive, but it also supports countless other tiny animals. Frogs, salamanders, snakes, snails, lizards, and a host of insects, spiders, and scorpions take refuge here. The water trapped in the leaves becomes a nutritious soup of rainwater, dirt, rotting leaves, animal droppings, decomposing insects, and plant juices that will nourish both the bromeliad and the critters that take refuge within its leaves. Yummmm!

I Live in the Glades

tance to the Everglades. When the rains stop and the Glades begin to dry up, alligators dig swimming holes. As they dig, they use their tails and snouts to pile vegetation and mud on the sides of their holes. Willows and other plants grow in the mud and rotting plants piled around the sides.

The alligator digs to provide itself with water and a well-stocked pantry for the coming dry season. In doing so, it provides the same for many other species. The gator holes become microcosms of life in the Glades. Fish and crustaceans take refuge in the holes. Many varieties of birds feed on the fish and crustaceans and nest in the shrubs around the holes. Other animals also feed on the fish, birds, and plants. Therefore, the alligator's swimming hole becomes a sanctuary for many species. They would not survive the dry winter without the food and water provided by the alligator.

Life is not easy in the condensed world of a gator hole. Many of the creatures there will become dinner for the alligator or another predator. Some will die as water levels drop and oxygen in the remaining water is depleted. Still, some of each species will survive until spring. When the spring rains come, the gator hole overflows its banks. Little fish, crustaceans, amphibians, and microorganisms spread out to repopulate the Everglades. Birds, reptiles, and mammals also extend their feeding and nesting grounds out into the fresh growth of spring. The wet season is a time of plentiful food and rapid growth. If the alligators die or leave a hole, it becomes stagnant and clogged with debris and eventually dries up.

The nest building habit of female alligators also benefits plants and other animals. In early summer, the female builds a mound nest of damp vegetation and mud. The

Biologist Dr. Jeff Schmid checks out a gator hole located in a wet prairie in the Picayune State Forest.

This crèche of baby alligators stays close to mama for protection from predators. Baby alligators are about eight or nine inches long when they are born and can grow to as much as 1000 pounds and almost 20 feet.

I Live in the Glades

mound raises the eggs above water level. The female lays from 30 to 50 eggs in a hole in the top of her mound and covers the hole with vegetation. The finished nest may be more than three feet high (just over a meter) and twice as wide. The nest provides a cozy home above water level for a variety of insects and invertebrates. Sometimes a raccoon or other animal makes a tasty meal of the eggs—but at the risk of being eaten by the mother alligator. A red-bellied turtle sometimes lays its own eggs within the nest structure. The turtle leaves and the mother alligator unknowingly cares for both sets of eggs.

Once the eggs are ready to hatch, the mother uses her front legs and jaws to open the nest. As the eggs hatch, she carries about ten babies at a time to the water. She pulls her tongue down to make room for them to sit in her mouth. Juveniles form a crèche—in biology, a nursery tended by a female animal—and stay close to the mother for about a year.

The alligator is a keystone species. In architecture, a keystone is the central wedge-shaped stone that holds an arch together. If the keystone is pulled out, the arch collapses. Similarly, a keystone animal or plant is one whose removal would cause the ecosystem to fail. Without the alligator, the delicate balance of the Everglades would be disrupted and many species would not survive. When alligators almost disappeared from the Everglades, their position as a keystone of the ecosystem became clear.

At one time alligators were hunted to make leather from their tough, beautiful hides. Farmers, who wanted to clear the land but feared the big reptiles, killed many more. As their numbers dwindled, conservationists saw the effect it was having on the ecosystem. They lobbied for laws to protect the alligator, but with little success. Finally, the

Buzz Off!

Anyone who has visited the Everglades has likely had a close encounter with the most ferocious of Everglades beasts—the mosquito. Although there are 43 species of mosquitoes in Everglades National Park, only 13 of them bite humans. That is enough, however, to make a stroll on the trails and boardwalks an itchy event. The female *Ochlerotatus taeniorhynchus*, pictured below emerging from its pupal case onto the water's surface, is known for being a pest to humans.

The annoying little insects are more than a nuisance though; they are a very important part of the Everglades food chain. Tree frogs, lizards, snakes, fish, birds, and dragonflies feed on mosquitoes. In addition, mosquito larvae, called wrigglers, are a favorite food of gambusia and killifish. These tiny fish are in turn eaten by fresh- and saltwater fish such as bass, tarpon, snook, redfish, and catfish. Egrets, spoonbills, woodstorks, and other birds also consume thousands of mosquito-eating fish.

If you hike in the Glades, wear light-colored clothing, long sleeves, long pants, socks, and a hat. If you still get bitten, just consider it a contribution to the Everglades food chain. Take comfort in the fact that Everglades mosquitoes do not carry malaria.

Endangered Species Act of 1973 prohibited the sale or possession of products from endangered species like the alligator. When it was no longer of economic value, the alligator began to reclaim its vital position in the ecosystem. Today the alligator is again a common sight in the Everglades, and is busy doing its part to protect the ecosystem.

The story of the alligator is just one example of interwoven relationships that make an ecosystem work. And, as with the alligator, the importance of a seemingly insignificant plant or animal is often not understood until it is too late, or almost so.

Periphyton

Another key player in the Everglades ecosystem is periphyton. Periphyton is not big and dramatic-looking like the alligator. In fact, it is yucky-looking. Periphyton is a scummy mass, formed by many varieties of algae and microscopic organisms clumped together, that grows abundantly in the Everglades. It clings to and covers submerged plants, rocks, and other surfaces. Its beauty may not be easy to see, but the role periphyton plays in life in the Everglades is beautiful. Periphyton is the base of the food chain. Insect larvae and other invertebrates, as well as larval frogs (tadpoles), salamanders, and other small creatures, eat periphyton. They in turn become food for small fish, frogs, and other small vertebrates, which then are eaten by bigger fish or birds. The large fish and birds are eaten by even larger predators such as alligators, bobcats, and Florida panthers. Providing food is not periphyton's only job. It also helps many insects and aquatic animals

survive the dry season. As the wetland dries out, the mats of periphyton settle to the bottom with the dying plants. Insects and aquatic invertebrates lay their eggs in the moist mats. Throughout the dry season, the spongy mass holds enough moisture to enable the eggs and some small creatures to survive. When the rains come, the eggs hatch and the tiny creatures spread out through the newly wet environment. Periphyton also removes excess calcium from the water. The calcium drops to the bottom and forms a layer of calcium-based mud called marl. Sawgrass and other marsh grasses need the marl to grow. In addition, periphyton releases oxygen into the air during the day and carbon dioxide at night, and when it dies it rots and builds new soil. In these ways, this unattractive composite of tiny organisms plays a large and dramatic role in life in the Everglades.

The River of Grass

The signature plant of the Everglades is sawgrass. The vast sawgrass prairies inspired Marjory Stoneman Douglas's description of the Everglades as the "River of Grass." It is a good description, even though sawgrass is not really a grass at all. It is a sedge. Grass has round, hollow stems, while sedges usually have solid, triangular stems. To distinguish a sedge from a grass, remember that sedges have edges. And in the case of sawgrass, those edges are wicked. They have tiny, upward-pointing saw teeth that can slice into bare skin.

Standing on an observation deck in Everglades National Park, you can see saw-

Appearances can be deceiving. In the wet season, periphyton clings to underwater stems and floats listlessly on top of the water (below). In the dry season, it coats the exposed ground. It looks like something gone bad, but is the base of the Everglades food chain and performs other important functions in the environment as well.

I Live in the Glades

Great White Egret

The great white egret (*Ardea alba*) is the largest egret in most of the world, but in the Everglades, the rare white form of the great blue heron is larger. The terms egret and heron are sometimes used interchangeably, but egrets are white herons and usually have long plumes in breeding season. Thus, the great blue heron is not an egret, but its white form is considered an egret. The great white egret stands 37 to 41 inches tall (94 to 104 cm) and has a wingspan of 52 to 57 inches (131 to 145 cm).

grass stretching to the horizon. Here and there, a tree island breaks the flat prairie or a slough cuts a meandering path. There are other grasses and plants mixed in, but most of what you see is sawgrass. The sawgrass holds the soil in place, regulates the flow of the water, cleanses it of impurities, and provides food for some animals and nesting or hiding places for others. The sawgrass remains the dominant plant in the prairies because it is ideally adapted to the pattern of water, drought, and fire that has defined the area.

Other threads in the Everglades tapestry

The Everglades is an environment rich in plant and animal life. Forty-five species of mammals, including several marine species, live in the Everglades. The alligator is joined by more than 50 other species of reptiles and approximately 20 species of salamanders, frogs, and toads. Scientists have recorded almost 350 species of birds in the Everglades. Countless species of butterflies, insects, spiders, snails, and other terrestrial invertebrates make their home there. Hundreds of species of fish and thousands of marine, estuarine, and freshwater invertebrates live in the waters of the ecosystem. Each species plays a role in maintaining the health of the system.

The water

The natural elements of an ecosystem are also vital players in making it all work. Of all of the elements of the Everglades, water plays the key role. The story of the Everglades is really the story of the water, because it defines the system and makes it unique. The water flow varies, and in the winter much of the Everglades dries up. But that is the nature of the Everglades. Individual plants and animals may die, but species have found ways to survive. Numbers are depleted in the winter, but spring rain brings new life. When the water quality or pattern of flow changes, the effects are devastating.

For example, the huge acreage devoted to agriculture puts increased amounts of phosphorus and nitrogen in the water. These are natural elements in the environment, but unnatural amounts are used in agriculture and the runoff drains into the Everglades. The Everglades is oligotrophic, which means that it has unusually low levels of nutrients. The life forms in the ecosystem are adapted to this low-nutrient environment and cannot adjust to the highly enriched water from the farms. For example, where levels of these chemicals are high, the sawgrass is crowded out and replaced by nutrient-hungry cattails.

Canals and drainage change the water flow pattern. Changes in the flow patterns have many effects, none of them good for the Everglades ecology. A few examples will illustrate the importance of the amount and timing of the water flow. Too much water may flood nesting grounds and feeding grounds. As Larry Ogren explains, "If the water is too deep it spreads fish and crustaceans over a larger area, causing wading birds to have a hard time finding food. As the water gets even deeper, the long legs of the birds are not long enough to allow them to feed by wading." On the other hand, if the land is allowed to dry, many fish die. When the birds cannot catch enough fish, they may not breed at all. If they have already bred, the hatchlings may starve. Some birds travel long distances from their nests to find food. If the distance is too far, they cannot bring back enough food to feed their chicks.

Cypress trees also depend on the right water levels to reproduce. Cypress seeds need to be under water for a period of time, but must eventually settle on solid ground to sprout. If the ground is too dry, they cannot go through their soak cycle. If it is too wet, there is no place to settle and sprout.

Estuaries are coastal fish factories that depend on the inflow of fresh water. Too much fresh water, however, causes oyster reefs, coral reefs, clam beds, and seagrass to die. Thus, the food chain is broken and commercial fisheries are destroyed.

This is life in the Everglades. Too little or too much water, or water at the wrong time causes native species to die off and allows exotic species to take over. Either extreme can kill the Glades. Without healthy water flow, the tapestry of the Everglades will disintegrate.

Chapter 3

Extinct, Endangered, and Exotic
The Three E's of Environmental Decline

It's not just species on islands or in rain forests or just birds or
big charismatic mammals, it's everything and it's everywhere. . . .
It is a worldwide epidemic of extinctions.

—Stuart Pimm

The wood stork (*Mycteria americana*), one of the largest wading birds in North America, stands as much as 45 inches tall (1.14 m) and has a wingspan of up to 65 inches (1.65 m). The snap of its bill on a fish is one of the fastest reactions in nature. In the 1930s there were approximately 60,000 wood storks in North America, but today there are only about 9,000. Because of this decline in population the wood stork was listed as a federally endangered species in 1984.

he health of the Everglades ecosystem is declining. Some
species have become extinct while others are endangered
or threatened. New species have moved in and staked claim
to the remaining habitat.

The Endangered Species Act (ESA) of 1973 and the Convention
of International Trade in Endangered Species of Wild Fauna and Flora
(CITES) protect wildlife and habitats. Nevertheless, the Everglades and
other sensitive ecosystems are still declining. The Endangered Species Act also made people aware of the effects of lost species on an
ecosystem. It called for the protection of all species. The ESA identifies
declining species as endangered or threatened. The Florida Department
of Environmental Protection has added a category—species of special
concern. This classification brings attention to a species before its numbers drop dangerously low. The World Conservation Union (IUCN)
has still different categories and maintains an international Red List of
Threatened Species. However, even with concerned organizations and
sound laws in place, political and commercial interests often sidetrack
good intentions.

Extinct

Extinct means gone. Forever. Throughout Earth's history species have
faded into extinction. Ecosystems slowly change over millennia and
the life forms they support also change. Some species vanish as others
better suited to the new conditions evolve. It is a normal part of life on
Earth.

Occasionally mass extinctions have occurred. The best known is
the "great dying" that wiped out the dinosaurs. Dinosaurs were large, strange-looking creatures and they left behind giant bones as evidence of their life. They have become media
darlings. Every three-year-old knows about dinosaurs. But they were only part of the story.

I Live in the Glades

Limpkin

Once abundant in Florida, the limpkin (*Aaramus guarauna*) was almost wiped out by humans hunting for food. Loss of apple snail habitat has also contributed to the decline of the species. The limpkin's bill is uniquely designed for feeding on apple snails. Closed, the bill has a gap just before the tip that makes it work like tweezers. The tip is also curved slightly to the right so it can easily slip into the right-handed chamber of the snail. The apple snail is disappearing from the Everglades, but it has been introduced in other parts of the world and is becoming a major pest as an exotic species. In the Everglades, the limpkin and the snail kept each other in balance until humans changed the habitat.

More than 50% of the species on earth at that time became extinct over a relatively short period of time.

According to DinoBuzz, a website sponsored by the University of California at Berkeley's Museum of Paleontology: "We know of several mass extinctions in the history of life; the great dying is not nearly the largest! The largest would be the "Permo-Triassic" extinction, between the Permian and Triassic periods, of the Paleozoic and Mesozoic eras. In this obviously catastrophic event, life on Earth nearly was wiped out—an estimated 90% of all species living at that time were extinguished."

Natural disaster caused these mass extinctions. For example, scientists believe that a giant meteorite slammed into Earth 65 million years ago. The impact caused the extinction of the dinosaurs and most of the other life on the planet. According to environmentalist Stuart Pimm, that was the fifth and most recent mass extinction. Pimm believes that the earth is facing a sixth mass extinction. He explains in a *National Geographic* magazine article: "Today the Earth is again in extinction's grip—but the cause has changed. The sixth extinction is not happening because of some external force. It is happening because of us, *Homo sapiens*, an "exterminator species," as one scientist has characterized humankind. The collective actions of humans—developing and paving over the landscape, clear-cutting forests, polluting rivers and streams, altering the atmosphere's protective ozone layer, and populating nearly every place imaginable—are bringing an end to the lives of creatures across the Earth."

Human technology, agriculture, and vanity

have sped up processes that once took millions of years. Humans have the skills and tools to cause radical change. In order to feed, house, and clothe a growing population, humans have brought huge changes to the Everglades. These changes have already resulted in extinctions as well as sharp declines in the numbers of other species.

On June 16, 1987, the last dusky seaside sparrow died. Orange Band, the last of the duskies, died in captivity at Disney World. It is the only animal whose exact date of extinction is known. The dusky's close relative, the Cape Sable seaside sparrow, is endangered. These two related birds show the importance of the seaside sparrow as an indicator species of marsh habitats. Environmental indicators are species that offer a signal of the biological condition in a watershed or ecosystem. They are a red flag warning that something is going wrong that will eventually affect the entire ecosystem.

Seaside sparrows live and nest in marsh grasses. They nest low where the grass is strong enough to support their nests. Unnaturally high water will drown their hatchlings. High water also makes it easier for snakes and turtles to rob their nests. In order to make dry land for building, water is diverted into the sparrows' nesting grounds. The sparrows suffer from loss of habitat, rising water caused by drainage for construction, and—prior to 1972, from the use of DDT to control mosquitoes on the construction site. DDT caused thinning of egg shells, making them very fragile and vulnerable. In 1972 DDT was banned for most uses

in the United States, but was still allowed for mosquito control to protect public health. The ban, with the public health exception, has since been adopted worldwide.

Endangered and nearly so

Endangered means nearly extinct. Threatened means nearly endangered. In Florida, a species of special concern is one that deserves monitoring because its numbers are declining or it needs a highly specific habitat. In the Everglades National Park, there are 14 endangered species, nine threatened species, and numerous species of special concern.

The Florida panther

The Florida panther is one of the most endangered animals on earth. In the 1990s, there were only 30 to 50 individual panthers remaining. Many of those showed signs of inbreeding and disease.

The panther is a flagship species of the Everglades. A flagship species is one that can capture the public's interest and concern. Publicity of a few flagship species brings support that helps the entire ecosystem. Conservation is not about single species, but about habitats. A healthy habitat maintains all of the species and relationships of the system.

The Florida panther is an ideal flagship species because it is large, charismatic, and a little frightening. On a poster, a panther grabs your attention. A picture of a snail or a marsh grass is just not as exciting. Yet support for the panther benefits every plant and creature living in its habitat.

The Panther: Friend or Foe?

As the Florida panther (*Felis concolor coryi*) inches its way back from the brink of extinction, it faces some new problems. A few panthers have attacked livestock, making some residents fear that they might also attack humans.

No one wants to feel that his or her children are in danger. However, the panther is a natural part of the environment of south Florida and it plays an important role in the ecosystem. There has never been a documented attack on a human by a Florida panther.

Our ancestors, who settled in rural America, knew the dangers of the land and protected their children and taught them to protect themselves. Today, city dwellers must protect their children from traffic and human predators. People who live near the water must protect their children from drowning. Citizens of areas where there are large predatory animals, such as cougars, bears, or wolves, have the same responsibility to protect their children from the unlikely possibility of attack. In a diverse, healthy environment, it is not possible to eliminate all dangers or to legislate safety.

This western cougar lives at Homosassa State Wildlife Park. She was a captive animal that was rescued and brought to the park. She can no longer support herself in the wild because her claws and fangs have been removed; therefore, she is a permanent resident at the park. These cougars are almost identical to the Florida panther. Western panthers have been imported into the state to strengthen the gene pool and save the Florida panther from extinction.

The Florida panther is one of more than 20 subspecies of cougar. The big cat's solid color varies from yellow to red to gray and allows it to blend into the landscape of either open prairie or forest. Its long tail—about two-thirds the length of its head and body—helps the panther balance as it leaps for prey. Males average about seven feet in length (2.13 meters), including the tail, and weigh about 120 pounds (54.5 kilograms). Females are slightly smaller.

In 1995, biologists released eight female Texas cougars into the Everglades to broaden the gene pool. The Texas cougar is the Florida panther's closest relative. There are only very slight differences between the Texas subspecies and the Florida panther. Since the Texas cougars were introduced, the number of panthers has increased to between 90 and 100. The introduction was very controversial because some people believe that the cross-bred animals are no longer true Florida panthers. However, without increasing the gene pool, the panther was destined to become extinct.

The last of the Florida panthers live on government and private protected lands in south Florida. The greatest threat to the panther's survival is loss, degradation, and fragmentation of its habitat. Panthers need a lot of space to survive, and they need to be able to move through it without passing through a parking lot or condominium swimming pool. A male panther may range over more than 200 square miles (520 square kilometers) and does not share its range with other males.

The panther is a predator. It eats young deer and other small animals. This may sound like a bad thing for the deer, but it is not. When the large predators disappear from an ecosystem, the remaining animals multiply rapidly. Eventually the population outgrows the food supply. Instead of a managed number of sleek, healthy animals, there are many animals weakened by hunger and disease. Therefore, the panther's dining habits help maintain a healthy balance of species in the ecosystem.

The wood stork

The wood stork (*Myteria americana*), another Everglades endangered species, has focused attention on water flow problems. The wood stork, one of the largest wading birds in the United States, stands more than three feet tall (0.9 meters). Its white feathered body topped by a featherless black head has earned it nicknames such as ironhead and preacher. When the wood stork opens its five-foot wingspan, it displays a fringe of iridescent greenish-black feathers.

The wood stork has been on the endangered list since 1984. According to the Everglades National Park website: "Their feeding behavior explains their predicament. Wood storks feed not by sight but by touch, "tacto-location," in shallow and often muddy water full of plants. . . . Walking slowly forward the stork sweeps its submerged bill from side to side. Touching prey, mostly small fish, the bill snaps shut with a 25 millisecond reflex action, the fastest known for vertebrates."

A pair of wood storks needs 440 pounds (200 kg) of fish in a breeding season.

gopher tortoise

Florida cooter

Turtles and Tortoises

Eleven species of fresh water turtles and five marine turtles live in Everglades National Park. Most of the freshwater species, such as the Florida cooter (*Pseudemys floridana*) shown here, live in marshes, sloughs, ponds, and solution holes. The Florida softshell turtle (*Apalone ferox*) shown here can be easily identified by its tough leathery shell and long pointed nose. It can grow to be 24 inches long (61 cm), and likes freshwater marshes and ponds.

Box turtles and gopher tortoises prefer the dryer environment of pinelands and hardwood hammocks. The gopher tortoise (*Gopherus polyphemus*) shown here is listed as a federally threatened species. It lumbers along on land, but is a master tunnel digger. Its burrows may be up to 35 feet (10.6 meters) and many other animals depend on the burrows for a place to hide or live.

All of the marine turtles in the Everglades are endangered or threatened.

softshell turtle

Kemp's ridley sea turtle

In the air, the awkward-looking wood storks are transformed. They use thermals to gracefully soar thousands of feet high and descend in a joyful series of dips, dives, and rolls. Wood storks often travel as much as 80 miles from nesting to feeding areas. If the fishing is not good, they may not have the strength to feed themselves and bring back enough food for their hatchlings.

During a normal breeding season, seasonally drying wetlands force large numbers of fish into small areas of shallow water. Without this dry-out, the wood stork cannot capture enough food to raise a family. On the other hand, if conditions are too dry many fish die and there is not enough food available. When natural wetland cycles are upset, wood storks do not nest at all, or if they do, they cannot take care of their fledglings.

The wood stork is only one of many birds affected by changing conditions in the Everglades. Three other Everglades birds are endangered. Draining has destroyed apple snail habitat, the primary food of the **snail kite**. Likewise, loss of habitat and degradation of habitat have almost wiped out the **Cape Sable seaside sparrow**. To survive, the **red-cockaded woodpecker** needs pine forests kept open by fire. It has almost disappeared from the Everglades, but still occurs occasionally in Big Cypress Swamp. Its loss affects many other species. Red-cockaded woodpeckers excavate cavities in living pine trees, thereby providing essential cavities for other cavity-nesting birds and mammals, as well as some reptiles, amphibians, and invertebrates. Many other Everglades birds are listed as threatened species or species of special concern. Overall, bird populations in the Everglades have declined by 90 percent since the days of the plume hunters. Regarding the status of bird populations worldwide, Stuart Pimm writes:

"Birds are already going extinct 100 times faster than they should. Our past actions have already fatally wounded so many other species that the fatalities will soon occur 1000 times faster than they should. Our current activities will harm even more species."

Exotic species

While the Everglades native species struggle to survive, other species have moved in and set up housekeeping. Non-native species that come to the Everglades through some human activity are called exotic or introduced species. They arrive in several ways. Sometimes wildlife managers introduce new species as biological controls. For example, a beetle that eats melaleuca may be used to help control that destructive introduced plant. These efforts may have merit, but are controversial. They sometimes go awry and create problems in the ecosystem. The melaleuca beetle, for example, could expand its diet to include food needed by other species important to the ecosystem.

Discarded pets are also a source of exotic animals in the Everglades. People buy unusual pets that grow large or ferocious, or become more nuisance than pleasure. Then the owners release them in the Everglades, thinking they will have a good life there. Farmers and landscapers have brought many foreign plants to the area. As long as these new plants stay in cultivated areas they are not considered exotic plants. Some of these plants, however, adapt quickly to the new environment and spread into wild areas.

There are many exotic plants and animals in the Everglades. Most of them never reproduce, or they blend in without causing serious problems. However, a few, called invasive exotics, find that their new home is perfect for growth and reproduction. Their new environment lacks the diseases or predators that keep them in check in their native environment. Therefore, they can multiply rapidly, crowd out the natives, and gobble up the resources. They are particularly successful in areas where habitat changes are putting stress on native species.

Animals introduced to the Everglades include pythons, boa constrictors, parakeets, parrots, wild hogs, and a number of fish species. Some of them are invasive and create problems in several ways. They compete with native animals for food and nesting sites. They sometimes prey on sensitive species. Occasionally, they do physical damage; for instance, wild pigs damage native vegetation and archaeological sites.

The Burmese python is breeding in the Glades and has become a serious problem. Pythons grow to as long as 26 feet and can weigh more than 200 pounds. The big snakes eat warm-blooded animals and could become a major threat to Everglades species. Park employees removed more than 150 pythons found in or near Everglades National Park in 2005. It is, however, plant species that pose the biggest threat to the future of the Everglades.

The big three

Of the many exotic Everglades plant species, three pose the greatest threat and present the strongest resistance to control. Water-hungry melaleuca (*Melaleuca quinquenervia*), a tree native to Australia, first came into the Everglades in the 1890s as a landscape plant. Residents later planted it as a windbreak, and developers, wanting more dry land to develop, planted it to help drain the Everglades with its voracious appetite for water. Today melaleuca thrives on more than 450,000

From Burma with Love

What is an Asian snake doing in the Everglades? Since 2000, wildlife importers have legally brought more than a million pythons to the United States. More than half were sold to Miami-area pet stores. The Burmese python is one of the six largest snakes in the world and can grow to 25 feet long (8 meters) and weigh as much as 400 pounds (180 kilograms). A well-fed python can grow to as much as eight feet (2.4 meters) in the first year of its life. When the pet python begins eying the family dog as a tasty snack, it is time for the snake to go.

To many snake owners, dropping the snake off in the Everglades seems like the kindest way to end the relationship. But the gesture is not a kindness to the native wildlife of the Everglades. The python feels right at home in the warm, moist climate of the Everglades. With the possible exception of the alligator, it has no natural enemies. In a battle with a python, the alligator does not always win. The python is multiplying rapidly in the Everglades. Unchecked, it could become a major threat to a fragile ecosystem.

The Burmese python (*Python molurus bivittatus*) is a huge, beautiful snake, but it does not belong in the Everglades—nor does it belong in your home unless you are trained to care for a large snake. Pythons are wild animals that get very large and sometimes behave in unpredictable ways. If they are not securely enclosed and properly cared for, they can become a serious threat to other pets and humans. Released pythons are now breeding in the Everglades and have become a threat to native Everglades animals.

Moonflower

The moonflower (*Ipomoea alba convolvulaceae*) is an aggressive vine with stems 15 feet (4.5 meters) or more long; it often drapes over other vegetation, forming a dense mat. The flowers open mostly at night and can be seen glowing in the moonlight.

acres of the Everglades. In densely infested areas, there may be as many as 31,000 trees and saplings per acre. Sharon Rauch, a reporter for the *Tallahassee Democrat*, writes: "Chop down a melaleuca, for instance, and the stump will sprout back within weeks. Burn it or douse it with herbicide and two million seeds no bigger than a pinpoint explode into the air. Use the bark [trunk] as a fence post, and it'll grow roots. You can't even drown the dang thing—seeds can live up to six months underwater."

Melaleuca crowds out native plants. It has taken over thousands of acres of breeding, nesting, and feeding ground for native species. In addition, some biologists believe that it sucks up water at such a rate that it interferes with the natural flow of the water. Others are not convinced; they claim that melaleucas' water-absorption rate cannot be proven by available testing methods and may not be any greater than many other plants.

Heat-treated melaleuca is now being used as mulch. It doesn't contain arsenic, as some mulches do; it doesn't float when it rains; it saves valuable cypress trees from becoming mulch; and it rids Florida of some plant pests.

Brazilian pepper (*Schinus terebinthifolius*), a shrub sometimes inaccurately called Florida holly, is also running amuck in the Everglades. Birds and other wildlife help to spread Brazilian pepper. They eat its red berries and drop the seeds all over the Everglades. The berries make birds drunk and sometimes they die. Humans suffer from skin rash and breathing problems caused by substances produced by the plant. Brazilian pepper spreads rapidly and crowds out native species. Nesting birds are not attracted to its dense tangled branches. Brazilian pepper has spread beyond the Everglades. This invasive species now infests more than 700,000 acres in middle and southern Florida.

The third major plant pest in the Everglades is casuarina (*Casuarina equisetifolia*), or Australian pine. In the late 1800s, farmers planted casuarina as a windbreak. Later,

These invasive exotics are crowding out native species that provide food and nesting sites for wildlife. In addition, Brazilian pepper causes rashes and respiratory problems in humans. Biologists believe that melaleuca produces a chemical that is offensive to animals, causing even alligators to move away when melaleuca takes over.

Australian pine

Brazilian pepper

Melaleuca

developers used it to hold the spoil banks along drainage canals. This tree, now found throughout south Florida, invades areas damaged by storms and land clearing. Australian pines grow in dense stands with thick carpets of needles. Native plant seedlings cannot sprout through this thick groundcover. Habitat changes caused by casuarina affect several animal species, including the cotton rat, marsh rabbit, and gopher tortoise. The trees also encroach on the nesting places above the high-tide line of loggerhead sea turtles, green sea turtles, and American crocodiles.

Professionals and volunteers have contributed thousands of dollars and countless hours to the effort. They have, however, found no effective way to control the exotic plants and animals that have invaded the Everglades.

Realistically, humans are the ultimate exotic species. Humans have spread across the planet using sophisticated technology to make rapid changes to the natural landscape. In the Everglades, we humans have changed the land to make it suitable for development and agriculture. We have polluted the air and water, and over hunted, trapped, and fished the wildlife.

In addition, our dependence on fossil fuels is causing global warming. The glaciers are melting and sea levels are rising. Rising sea levels present a major threat to low-lying wetland areas such as the Everglades.

On the up side, with a sense of responsibility and stewardship of our planet, we can reverse much of the damage. We must make compromises and accept that we cannot use resources wastefully. *Homo sapiens* is the only species with the ability and technology to bring balance and harmony back to the planet. It is an awesome responsibility.

Small green iguanas that are sold as pets can grow to be four to six feet long. When they get big, or their owners tire of them, they are often released into the Everglades.

Marjorie

In 1989 boaters stopped to investigate what appeared to be a dead manatee. They saw deep gashes from boat propellers and were surprised to see the 1300-pound animal weakly lift her head and take a breath of air. The boaters reported the injured animal to park rangers, who took her to Miami Seaquarium's Animal Care Department where she was named Marjorie.

Marjorie slowly recovered from her injuries. She adopted Graham, an orphaned calf rescued near Key Largo, and in 1993 gave birth to a calf of her own, Valentine. Eventually the family of three moved to Homosassa Springs State Wildlife Park. In 1995 they were well enough to return to the wild and were released near the spot where Marjorie had been injured. The two calves were able to benefit from Marjorie's experience of living in the wild. Park officials continued to monitor their movements and saw all three become healthy members of Florida's endangered manatee population.

Chapter 4

The People of the Glades
From Grass Huts to Condos

Oh, they say hard times are coming again,
I hope I'm gone if and when.
We was down to bone and skin,
And I don't want to go through that again.
—the chorus of "Hard Times" by Glen Simmons

In the 1800s lacy white snowy egret *(Egretta thula)* plumes were highly prized for decorating ladies' hats. In 1886 their plumes were valued at $32 per ounce—more than twice the value of gold at the time! They were hunted almost to extinction before laws were passed and enforced to protect them and other beautifully plumed Everglades species.

South Florida is new land. The estimated age of the earth is more than four billion years, while south Florida became dry land only about 25,000 years ago. Humans have likely lived on the southern end of the peninsula less than half of that time.

Florida did not emerge from the seas as jagged peaks pushed up by volcanoes and torn apart by earthquakes. Instead, it formed gently in tune to the rise and fall of seawater. Through a series of ice ages, glaciers sucked up water as they formed. The sea level dropped, leaving a layer of shell and organic material on newly exposed land. When the glaciers melted, the sea level rose again, covering the land. When the sea level stabilized after the last ice age, the Florida peninsula remained above the sea. On the southern end of the peninsula, the land was very flat and tilted slightly to the southeast—just enough for water to flow slowly toward the end of the land. Along the edges, limestone ridges rose slightly higher, creating a shallow saucerlike basin in the center.

Plants and animals found their way south from the continent, while others came from the West Indies on floating debris or caught up in air currents. Thereby, the tip of the Florida peninsula became the northernmost range of many tropical species and the southernmost range of temperate species from the north. The mix created a diverse and unusual ecosystem.

Much of the land was under water most of the year. It was muggy and buggy. There were poisonous snakes, biting insects, and thick tangles of plants with briars or saw-toothed leaf edges. However, the fish and game were plentiful. There were wild fruits, berries, edible plants, and roots. So they came—the first human inhabitants of the Everglades.

The earliest evidence of humans living in the Glades dates back at least 10,000 years. Anthropologists once thought that they came from the West Indies. Today, most researchers believe that humans made their way southward over land. Like

I Live in the Glades

Purple Gallinule

This colorful wetlands bird has very long toes that help it walk on lily pads and other floating vegetation. The purple gallinule (*Porphyrula martinica*) also uses its feet to lift the edge of the lily pad and peer underneath to look for tasty invertebrates or plant tidbits. The purple gallinule is similar to the common moorhen, but much more colorful.

the other big mammals—such as the bear, panther, and deer—they were too big and heavy to travel on floating debris or air currents.

A number of tribal groups set up housekeeping along the edges of the Everglades. They are usually referred to collectively as the Glades Indians, but there were several separate tribes. By the time Europeans discovered Florida, the main tribes were the Tequesta along the east coast and the Calusa along the west coast.

Eventually, the Calusa greatly outnumbered and probably dominated the Tequesta. We know little about how these people lived because they left little behind. They made their tools, weapons, and building materials from shell or perishable materials such as hide, wood, and natural fibers. Much of what we know comes from shell middens where they tossed their garbage and broken pottery.

In addition, two things have given us an insight into their lifestyle. In 1545, thirteen-year-old Hernando D'Escalante Fontaneda survived a shipwreck on the south Florida coast. He lived with the Calusa for seventeen years before being rescued. When Fontaneda finally arrived in Spain, he wrote a rambling account of his life with the Indians. He wrote details about what they ate and how they dressed:

"They go naked except only some breech cloths woven of palms, with which the men cover themselves: the women do the like with certain grass that grows on trees. This grass looks like wool, although it is different from it. The common food is fish, turtle, and snails (all of which are alike fish) . . . Some eat sea-wolves [West Indian seal]; not all of them, for there is a distinction between the higher and the lower classes, but the principal persons eat them."

Fontaneda was not the first Spaniard to visit Florida but his life with the Indians provided a first-hand look into their lifestyle.

Another boost to our knowledge of the Calusa came in 1896 when the Pepper-Hurst archaeological expedition found many artifacts well-preserved in the peat of Marco Island. Peat, a compact mass of partially decomposed organic material, contains no oxygen. The lack of oxygen limits the microorganisms that can live in it, making it an excellent preservative for artifacts. The Marco Island findings included wooden objects, some with vividly colored paint still intact. They found ceremonial objects as well as tools and implements of daily life.

The first Europeans

Juan Ponce de Leon claimed Florida for Spain in 1513 and named it La Florida, which means "the flower." Ponce de Leon tried to colonize southwest Florida, but in 1521, Calusa warriors killed him. The Spanish built missions and tried to convert the Indians to Christianity. Eventually, the Spanish had enough of the hostile Indians, heat, snakes, mosquitoes, and tropical diseases. They decided that the Everglades was not a fit place to live and they left. Even so, their impact on the native peoples was dreadful. Many Indians died fighting the Spanish and others were taken into slavery. Even more fatal than Spanish guns, however, were the diseases the Europeans brought with them. The native people had no immunity to the European diseases and epidemics spread through their villages. The Calusa and all other indigenous Glades Indians disappeared from Florida in the 1700s.

Seminole and Miccosukee

Because European settlers did not respect the rights and humanity of the Native Americans already living on the land, conflict was inevitable. Most north Florida Indians of the 19th century were members of the Creek Nation, and in the 1830s the United States government forced most of the Creeks to move to a reservation in the territory of Oklahoma. Some of the Creeks refused to go and, with some African American runaway slaves, formed a new tribe called the Seminoles.

The Seminoles moved deeper into Florida to avoid being sent to Oklahoma. They farmed, raised cattle, and hunted. President Andrew Jackson was determined to rid Florida of Indians and tried again to move them west of the Mississippi. The Seminoles again refused to go. Jackson declared war on them.

Through two Seminole Wars, the Indians moved farther south and finally into the Everglades. They used the harsh wet terrain to their advantage in fights with the Army troops. After many lives were lost on both sides, the Army gave up and many of the Seminoles remained in the Everglades. The Florida Seminoles are the only American Indians who never signed a peace treaty with the United States.

The Miccosukee, descendants of a Muskogee Creek tribe, migrated from Tennessee and the Carolinas and formed a close alliance with the Seminoles in Florida even though they spoke a different language. For many years, the Seminoles and Miccosukee were lumped together as one group. Today, largely because of language differ-

This photograph of a Seminole village near Fort Myers was taken in about 1938. It shows the many activities of day-to-day life at the time.

ences, the Miccosukee are recognized as a separate tribe. The Seminoles and Miccosukee still live in the Everglades today. Though fiercely proud of their heritage, they have had to adopt many non-Indian ways. They are teachers, lawyers, laborers, farmers, and entrepreneurs—just like their neighbors. The Miccosukee own several tourist concessions along Highway 41 (the Tamiami Trail), where they sell airboat rides and souvenirs.

The Seminoles have grown from operating tax-free tobacco shops to being an up-and-coming force in international business. They opened a bingo hall in Fort Lauderdale, then expanded to casinos and other businesses. Although the tribe is also in the cattle and citrus businesses, 90 percent of their budget comes from gambling facilities. In 2006 they purchased Hard Rock

International, which brought them not only Hard Rock cafes, but Hard Rock hotels and casino resorts.

White settlers bring changes

In the early nineteenth century, white fishermen worked the southern coast of Florida. Salvage groups retrieved usable goods from ships sunk on the reefs, and a few military outposts protected shipping lanes. But almost nothing was known of the vast center of south Florida. It was impossible to take boats through the tangled mangrove jungle or far into the shallow waters of the sawgrass marsh. Wading through the muck was uncomfortable and slow. Sawgrass sliced exposed skin, black clouds of disease-carrying mosquitoes hung in the air, biting insects and spiders crawled everywhere. Travelers also feared the alligators, snakes, panthers, and

A-frogging They Did Go

A Glades skiff slides through the night, a glowing figure poised in the bow. Suddenly—a splash and a glint of gas light on iron. Another succulent pig frog (*Rana grylio*) is pulled from the gig and dropped into the bottom of the skiff. In the late 1800s and early 1900s, frog hunting was big business in the Everglades. The town of Fellsmere was known as the frog capital of Florida. Even today, Fellsmere celebrates its history with an annual frog leg festival.

Frogs were hunted at night. Before the advent of the airboat and battery-powered headlamps, frog hunters used wooden Glades skiffs and the time-tested, British-made carbide headlamp. The headlamps were fueled by powdered calcium carbonate that reacted with a drip of water from the two-part canister. The water served as a catalyst to produce acetylene gas. The gas was ignited by a flint striker on the edge of the polished metal reflector.

The skiff was long for stability, flat-bottomed for the shallow Glades waters, and narrow to fit through winding sloughs and tight openings in the vegetation. The frog hunter loaded his skiff with several days' provisions plus a large burlap bag containing a solid cake of ice packed in sawdust for insulation. He then poled the skiff into the wilderness and selected a suitable tree island for a base camp. There he buried the ice and covered it with a board to keep critters out. His "refrigeration unit" was ready for his catch of frogs. After dark, the hunter attached his lamp to his hat, lit it, and poled his skiff into the prairie. The light would reflect brightly from the frogs' eyes. It located the frog for the hunter and momentarily blinded and immobilized it for an easy capture with a multi-pronged gig.

A compass was almost useless in the dark, featureless environment of the Glades. The frog hunter navigated by the stars and their position relative to his tree island base camp. Back at the camp, he cleaned his frogs, keeping only the saddle of two connected legs, and packed them in the makeshift ice chest. The tired hunter then settled in under a mosquito shelter constructed of burlap or flour bags for a few hours of sleep.

The economy of the Fellsmere area was based largely on the frogging industry. Thousands of pounds of the succulent, pricy delicacies were shipped and served in fancy restaurants as far away as New York. Today, Fellsmere funds its youth activities with proceeds from the Frog Leg Festival, where you can enjoy a tasty frog leg dinner for just $8.00.

White Ibis

The white ibis (*Eudocimus albus*) uses its curved bill to probe in the mud for crustaceans and sometimes wanders from the water to search for insects in the grass. During breeding season the ibis's legs are brilliant red. The ibis is 22 to 27 inches tall (58 to 69 cm).

wolves. The wild heart of Florida remained unknown except to Indians.

However, as civilization pushed southward, homesteads and settlements began to appear on hammocks and mangrove islands. Renegades and outlaws came first. Families pushed by circumstance and drawn by opportunity followed them into the hostile environment.

Life was hard. Some settlers farmed or raised cattle in the northern Glades. Farther south hunting and trapping made more money. Bird plumes for ladies' hats, animal pelts for clothing, and alligator hides for shoes and bags were in high demand in northern cities and Europe. The pelt and alligator hide trades were almost sustainable, but the plume hunters wreaked havoc on bird populations.

In those days, flocks of thousands of birds would darken the sky as they passed overhead. The supply seemed endless. But the beautiful feathers coveted by hat designers were at their fullest and most colorful in breeding season, when hunting them was at its easiest. Birds gathered in huge rookeries to breed and raise their young. Hunters attacked the rookeries. They killed hundreds of birds and left nests of eggs and fledgling birds to die. At this rate of slaughter, it did not take long for bird populations to drop.

Life in the Everglades

There are not many written records of early life in the Everglades, but a few Gladesmen kept journals. Rob Storter's family came to the Glades in the 1830s. They owned all of what is now Everglades City, and they ran a freight and passenger business between communities. Storter kept a journal illustrated with his own drawings. He told about going with his dad to deliver goods and passengers:

"I accompanied my dad on many trips. Sometimes he would let me steer the boat when the weather was good. I'll never forget the mixture of smells that came from the deck of that boat when it was loaded and ready to sail. Families all over the Ten

Lighting the Way to Safety

South Florida settlements dotted the coastline because the vast sawgrass Everglades of the interior was almost impenetrable. Goods were moved from town to town by boat. Although travel by sea was easier than land travel, shallow waters, sandbars, and thousands of islands made navigating the coastal waters challenging. In 1884, the Sanibel Island lighthouse was built to help sailors safely reach the mainland port at Ft. Myers. Today, the city of Sanibel maintains the property and city employees live in the two keepers houses.

Thousand Islands brought their goods to my dad to be taken to the Keys and sold. ... Back then there was a family on every island that could be lived on, and everyone had something to sell. Aunt Toggie Brown, mama's sister, would send her hot pepper sauce and sell it for fifteen cents a bottle. They were the same peppers that were stuck to our tongues when we said a bad word. We'd pick guavas and get fifty to seventy-five cents a box for them. Joe Wiggins would send cabbages he grew. A man from Onion Key brought figs and grapes to sell.

Mr. McKinney sent redbirds; the Key West market paid fifty cents to $1.25 each for the birds. We carried five-hundred-pound boxes of salt pork, which sold for ten cents a pound. ... Late at night ... I'd hear papa singing "Amazing Grace" or another hymn and it seemed like he sang all night long. I'd hear the booms squeak, the noise of the water splashing against the sides of the boat—it was beautiful music ringing in my ears."

Glen Simmons kept his journal in the early 1900s, but life had changed little over the past hundred years. Simmons' family hunted alligators and fished for a living. Simmons remembers growing up in a tiny Everglades house:

"Pa built our house out of rough lumber that they got from Frazier's sawmill. That house wasn't tied down, it stood up off the ground on some wooden blocks. I guess they just depended on its weight to keep it grounded. It was a one-room house, about sixteen to eighteen feet long and twelve feet wide. We all slept on cots in there and sat on boxes or a trunk. The kitchen was in the corner and Ma cooked on a four-hole stove, which cost six dollars. Me and my middle brother, Alvin, sat on a trunk to eat at the table. That trunk had some long cracks in it. My brother knew just how to move so the crack would pinch my behind. He could look surprised when I hollered."

Simmons and his family huddled in the safety of a neighbor's small block storm-house while the 1926 hurricane washed their house off its foundation and dropped it on the edge of a glade. They never moved it back. He recalls that they had to carry water farther from the pump, but they could now fish from the porch. The storm also killed all of their chickens. "Ours were all dead and scattered out, but good to eat. That's when us young'uns got something besides neck, feet, and legs."

In his book on early life in the Everglades, Charlton Tebeau wrote that the people of the Ten Thousand Islands area and the mangrove coast lived

"... perched precariously on patches of land scarcely above normal high tides. This Florida frontier attracted and bred a particularly

Somewhere near Florida City, Glen Simmons poles his glades skiff through the Everglades. The photograph was taken sometime before 1992.

Tampa to Miami—It was a Long, Long Way

The media dubbed them the "Trail Blazers." They were 26 young men and eight Ford Model Ts, and they made the first automobile crossing of the southern Everglades. The state is a little more than 100 miles across at that point. In 1923 that meant three weeks of slogging through mud, swatting mosquitoes, pushing the cars, digging the cars out of the mud, swatting more mosquitoes, and cursing each other and the endless miles of mean, wet prairie.

While the Trail Blazers traveled, other young men were making the crossing as well. They were the road crews hard at work building the Tamiami Trail. They had already been on the job for ten years, and would toil for another five years before the new highway opened in 1928. Roan "Doc" Johnson, a surveyor, worked on the road for the final two years. "Doc" and his crew traveled by ox cart because the oxen could plod through the muck easier than horses or mules. He recalls setting up camp in the water because there was not enough dry ground for their bunks. There were advantages—he could wash his feet right from his bunk and the water provided a tight seal on his mosquito netting.

From 1924 until 1928 Meece Ellis operated the walking dredge. The dredge, aided by 2.5 million sticks of dynamite, dug the 25-foot-wide by 12-foot-deep (7.6 by 3.6 meters) canal that provided the fill to build up the road bed. In a ten-hour workday the dredge could dig out 80 feet of rock and muck—that is, if there were no major breakdowns or delays. Meece was proud to be a part of the road crew, in spite of hardships that included the ever-present dampness, mosquitoes, bedbugs, and the ten-gallon nail keg with top and bottom removed that served as a primitive toilet.

The road builders were right to be proud. The Tamiami Trail was a huge accomplishment and it opened up south Florida for development and commerce. Even today, the Tamiami Trail speeds travelers across the wild Everglades in air-conditioned comfort. Naples to Miami takes about two hours—unless you stop to view the wildlife or to enjoy Clyde Butcher's gallery of phenomenal photography. An amazing accomplishment, yet it did massive damage to the Everglades ecosystem by cutting off the sheet flow of the river of grass.

Osprey

The osprey (*Pandon haliaetus*), with a wingspan of 59–71 inches (150–180 cm), is one of the largest birds of prey in the United States. It is sometimes mistaken for the bald eagle, but the even larger eagle has a dark chest and underside and at maturity has an all white head. Live fish make up about 99 percent of the osprey's diet. Barbed pads on the soles of its feet help the osprey hold on to slippery fish. It carries large fish head-first to reduce wind resistance.

The osprey almost disappeared between 1950 and 1970, but since the ban on the pesticide DDT it has made a strong comeback in many areas. It is common in the Everglades. The osprey will readily nest on artificial structures and its large nests are often seen on telephone poles, channel markers, and nest platforms built for that purpose.

hardy type of men and women. They lived in such isolation that they were compelled to be self-sufficient and, indeed, it was precisely this isolation that attracted some people. Their only contact with each other and the outside world was by boat—in the early days a skiff propelled by oars, or perhaps a sailboat. They lived at the mercy of storm and high water, building and rebuilding homes that they knew would likely one day be destroyed."

In spite of hardships, the population of the Everglades grew. Developers and entrepreneurs with big dreams joined the homesteaders, hunters, and fishermen. They wanted to turn the Everglades into a paradise for farmers, ranchers, and business people. In Miami they saw the potential of the area as a tourist destination. Something had to be done about all that marshy, buggy land to make room for building dreams. Without the water, they thought, the Glades muck would make rich farming and grazing land and it would open up land for building houses, hotels, and businesses. Draining the Everglades would also reduce the risk of floods. In reality, rather than creating a paradise, removing the water would destroy a valuable and unique ecosystem. But they could not foresee the long-term effects of their efforts.

Developers promoted south Florida nationwide as a tropical paradise and the land boom was on. Investors bought land sight-unseen. Sometimes it was high and dry on the coastal ridge, but often it was deep in the Everglades and covered by water for half of the year. However, the south Florida economy was booming. There was quick money made buying and selling land. But much of the money was only on paper—deeds and mortgages. When the hurricane of 1926 ended the land boom, the Glades inhabitants were poorer than ever. Wealthy speculators went broke over night. There was no money to back up the paper deals. Simmons writes, "After the land boom bottomed out, we were so poor that the cat was afraid to bring a rat home. Finally it got afraid to come home."

After a few years, the terror of the hurricanes faded and more and more people came to vacation or make their homes in south Florida. Villages turned into towns and then into cities. Miami blossomed on the eastern coastal ridge and Ft. Myers and Naples sprawled along the west coast. Developments of hundreds of houses fringed the Glades. Hotels stood elbow to elbow along the coast, and eventually massive condominium complexes began springing up in what had once been wetlands. A growing population needed land for building and farming as well as water for household use, irrigation and industry. Canals crisscrossed the land and wetlands became dry land.

Chapter 5

An Ecosystem at Risk
It's All About the Water

*Natural places, ecosystems, are not fragile. They are, in the main, tough
as an old tire. The capacity of the earth for compensation and forgiveness
after repeated abuses has kept the planet alive, but it has also encouraged more abuse.*
—Randy Lee Loftis with Marjory Stoneman Douglas,
Afterword to *The Everglades: River of Grass, Revised Edition*

Canals that slice arrow-straight through the Everglades were intended to drain land for houses and farms and to prevent flooding. In the process they have almost destroyed the Everglades ecosystem by changing the flow and timing of the water.

he River of Grass has been dammed, ditched, dredged, diked, and drained. Nineteen hundred miles of canals slice across former wetland prairies. More than 200 gates and pumps control the passage of the water. Lake Okeechobee has been turned into a giant bathtub. Meandering rivers now run straight and narrow. Sugar cane, tomatoes, and citrus grow on hundreds of thousands of acres of former wetlands. High-rise condominiums, golf courses, and shopping malls have outgrown the high ground of the limestone ridges and spread into the drained wetlands.

It seemed like a good idea at the time. After the land bust and the hurricanes of the 1920s, Florida's economy needed a boost. South Florida was replumbed in the name of progress and meeting human needs. At first glance, it worked. Florida is a worldwide tourist destination, a retirement paradise, and a major producer of sugar, citrus, and vegetables. But the cost has been huge. To understand the price that Florida is paying for economic success, you have to understand wetlands. Specifically, you have to understand the role the Everglades plays in south Florida ecology.

The value of wetlands

A wetland is land that stays wet all or part of the year. There are many types of wetlands. Each has its own hydrology—or water conditions. The Everglades includes several types of wetland—swamp marsh, mangrove jungle, and estuary—but its sheet flow hydrology is unique. Wetlands produce some of the most diverse plant and wildlife populations on earth. Wildlife, however, is only part of the overall value of these soggy habitats.

Wetlands allow floodwaters to spread harmlessly over a large area, and they absorb

I Live in the Glades

Tarpon

Tarpon live in warmer coastal waters and can tolerate variations in salinity. They often wander into bays and even upriver to fresh water. The tarpon has very little food value for humans, but is a popular game fish because of its large size and ability to jump. The largest tarpon ever caught in Florida was 243 pounds (110 kg). Most anglers release the fish after catching it, although no one is sure what the survival rate is for released fish. The Florida Marine Research Institute is designing a study to learn how many released tarpon survive. The tarpon is easy to identify due to its upturned mouth and unusually large tough scales. Adult tarpon eat shrimp, crabs, and fish, and are in turn eaten by sharks and sometimes dolphin and alligators. Unlike most fish, tarpon go through a larval stage. Both the eggs and the ribbonlike larvae are an important food source for birds and small fish.

much of the impact of storms. Wetlands also remove pollutants from the water, and fresh water from wetlands joins the salt water of the sea to create estuary breeding grounds for fish and shellfish. In addition, water evaporates from the wetlands and falls again as rain or seeps through the ground to recharge groundwater supplies. This is, perhaps, the most important role of the Everglades.

Turn the tap and water comes out. As long as water appears on demand, most people do not think about where it came from or how it got there. Most of the water supply for south Florida comes from the Biscayne Aquifer—a layer of porous rock and sand that holds groundwater. The Everglades feeds the aquifer. Much of the Everglades water never reaches the sea. It evaporates and falls again as rain or it seeps into the ground to become part of the aquifer. Archie Carr explains how the Everglades recharges the aquifer and why it matters: "The peculiar properties of this floor of fissured rock, covered and calked by muck, bear as much on the welfare of man in Miami as they do on otters and Everglades kites. The rock is the aquifer—the underground water storage and delivery system— for the Gold Coast's wells. The recharging

During the dry winter months much of the Everglades becomes dry grassland, but spring rains bring new life.

of this system depends on the capacity of the muck to hold water. The muck in turn is the debris of an integrated biological community that is dependent upon protracted flooding. . . . There could be no more graphic proof of the interdependence of man and nature than the predicament of the metropolitan lower east coast of Florida. There, for decades, agricultural and urban development has been progressively destroying the hydrologic system that makes life possible both in the Everglades and in the cities. The realization of that fact is the greatest single hope for saving any wilderness in southern Florida, and perhaps for saving the cities themselves."

With the threat of global warming, wetlands grow even more important. Scientists believe that increased carbon dioxide in the atmosphere is the main cause of global warming. Burning fossil fuels releases carbon dioxide into the air. Plants and soil—especially peat soil—absorb carbon dioxide from the air. Recent studies show that wetlands may store as much as 40 percent of earth's terrestrial carbon. Thereby, wetlands may slow the rate of global warming. On the other hand, draining wetlands releases large amounts of carbon dioxide and increases the rate of global warming.

Over the next 100 years, rising temperatures may cause climate changes. The changes may include more frequent storms, rising sea levels, and higher surface water temperatures. Wetlands can help protect populated areas from these effects. Most

I Live In the Glades

String Lily

Many wildflowers grow in the Everglades. They grow in the sun-washed prairies, as a flash of color from the murky depths of the swamp, or floating on the surface of ponds and sloughs.

The string lily or swamp lily (*Crinum americanum*) glows from the shadows of the swamp. The string lily's stout stalk lifts its flowers above a bed of glossy green leaves.

of south Florida, however, is only a few feet above sea level and is already feeling the effects of rising sea levels. Coastal areas are eroding and the mangrove forests are beginning to move inland—reducing the size of the freshwater Everglades.

Saltwater seepage into the aquifer is already a problem. As the Everglades wetland gets smaller, it is less able to recharge the aquifer and hold back the sea water. Hence, even slight changes in sea level will have a huge effect on the already struggling Everglades.

When people think of the decline of the Everglades they usually think of threatened wildlife. In reality, the lifestyle of all of south Florida, both human and wild, is threatened. How did it come to this?

Draining the Everglades

In the late 1800s and early 1900s the coast of south Florida was lovely. Palms and tropi-

cal flowers lined beautiful beaches. However, there was only a narrow strip of dry land along the coast. In the middle there was dense, buggy marsh. Developers and politicians looked toward the Everglades and saw opportunity. "Drain it! Make it useful!" they cried.

In 1881 Hamilton Disston, a wealthy Philadelphia businessman, bought four million acres from the state of Florida. He planned to prove that the Everglades could be drained. He also planned to get richer by growing sugar cane and selling drained acreage for development. After devoting ten years and a lot of money to the project, Disston went home and committed suicide. He had dredged a canal between the Caloosahatchee River and Lake Okeechobee. Another eleven-mile canal stretched from the lake into the northern Everglades. However, he had only drained about 80,000 acres. Disston was financially ruined, but, with 80,000 acres of newly dry land, he proved that the Everglades could be drained.

Napoleon Bonaparte Broward, a former riverboat captain and gunrunner, ran for governor in 1904. He promised to drain "that pestilence-ridden swamp" and build an empire. As governor, Broward added to the growing system of canals and drainage ditches, but he died in 1910 before he saw his empire completed.

A hurricane dealt a crippling blow to Miami in 1926. Two years later an even more destructive storm washed out the muck dam on the southern end of Lake Okeechobee. More than 2,000 people died in the resulting flood. After the hurricanes, work in the Everglades continued but the focus changed. People were afraid. They wanted protection from floods.

In 1947 more flooding threw flood control and water management into high gear with the Army Corps of Engineers in charge. After years of labor and expense, dikes and locks circled Lake Okeechobee. Huge pumps controlled water coming into or out of the lake. It was as simple as draining or filling a huge bathtub. In addition to taming the lake, the Corps turned the vast wetland into a network of numbered canals. The seasonal water flow pattern of the Everglades was cut off.

The roads

The Tamiami Trail—the last 275 miles of US Hwy 41—connects Tampa with Miami. The Trail shoots south from Tampa to Naples through congestion, traffic, and aggravation that would do any metropolitan highway

in the world proud. Then it takes an abrupt eastward turn toward Miami. This part of the trail slashes through miles of mostly uninhabited Everglades. Traffic thins out and alligators, wading birds, and mosquitoes replace gas stations and strip malls.

The Trail was completed in 1928. It was a phenomenal engineering feat—a monument to ingenuity and perseverance. One large step for humankind—one major disaster for the Everglades. Huge dredges and two and a half million sticks of dynamite broke up the bedrock. The rock and muck were dredged from the north side of the road bed and piled up to raise the road above water level. The result was a raised road with a trench running beside it. The trench is called the Tamiami canal. The meager sheet flow that still slides across the northern Glades drains into the canal. A few culverts and bridges channel water into the southernmost Everglades, but the sheet flow that sustained the system is lost.

Alligator Alley, built in the 1960s, was the second road to run east-west across the southern Everglades. Built as State Road 84, Alligator Alley was re-engineered in the 1980s as part of Interstate 75. The new highway, which runs through the Florida Panther National Wildlife Refuge, has had an impact on the Everglades, but not as severe as the Tamiami Trail. The disruption of the water flow is less complete due to long bridges and wildlife underpasses.

Canal-38—the ditch

The Kissimmee River project was the ultimate insult to the suffering ecosystem. The

Kissimmee twisted snakelike across central Florida to Lake Okeechobee. For several months of each year, the river spread out of its banks across a huge floodplain. Countless fish and birds made their home in and around the river and the wetlands it created. The Kissimmee was one of the most beautiful and productive rivers in America. The Kissimmee supplied more than 50 percent of Lake Okeechobee's water and therefore, it played an important role in the health of the entire Everglades ecosystem.

Ranchers and builders wanted flood control and more dry land to build houses and graze cattle. They pushed Congress to "fix" the river. The Kissimmee was turned over to the Army Corp of Engineers in spite of predictions by conservationists that the project would ruin the river.

The Corps turned a 103-mile-long, six-foot-deep, scenic river into a 56-mile, stick-straight, 30-foot-deep canal. They renamed it C-38. People called it the ditch. Ditch was a good description because the river died. Water birds declined by 92 percent, bald eagles by 74 percent. Oxygen levels in the water dropped and the fish died. Storm water could no longer spread across the floodplain. Polluted water poured into the canal without first filtering through cleansing wetlands. The ditch dumped tons of nutrient-rich, polluted water directly into Lake Okeechobee.

Lake Okeechobee

The "liquid heart of Florida," the second biggest lake wholly in the United States, has no waterfront. For a lake view you must drive or climb to the top of a grassy, sloping wall of earth. Once on top you cannot go far without running into a barrier.

The wall, or levee, protects the surrounding communities from flooding and supplies irrigation water to farms. At least, that was the plan—but the levee is old now and beginning to leak. Memories of Hurricane Katrina's assault on the levees of New Orleans in 2005 make residents glance uneasily toward the lake when a storm approaches.

Canals dump water rich in phosphates into the walled-off lake, causing algal blooms. Water levels in the lake are usually either higher or lower than they were naturally. Either extreme creates problems. Too much water puts stress on the levee and also causes submerged plants to die, which in turn eliminates fish habitat. Too little water allows exotic plants, such as melaleuca, to thrive and crowd out native species. In extreme cases the lake bottom can burn, killing even more native plants.

In 2007 persistent drought led to wildfires across Florida and Georgia and brought lake levels approximately 13 feet (four meters) below normal. Thousands of acres of dry, exposed aquatic plants burned.

When the water is high, huge pumps dump excess water into canals and from there into the Caloosahatchee and St. Lucie Rivers. The Caloosahatchee runs to the Gulf coast and the St. Lucie to the Atlantic. The influx of phosphate-laden fresh water is killing the bays.

Imposing floodgates and locks regulate the flow of water from Lake Okeechobee. Water no longer flows naturally from the lake into the Everglades

A lakeside park in Clewiston offers views of water control machinery, but to see the lake, you must climb to the top of the dike.

Everglades Agricultural Area

Originally water spilled out of Lake Okeechobee into thousands of acres of custard apple swamp. Custard apple is a subtropical fruit tree common to swampy areas. From there the lake water slid slowly southward in a wide shallow sheet. The black peat soil beneath the surface was so rich in organic material that when allowed to dry it would burn. Perfect soil for farming—or so it seemed.

Seven hundred thousand acres of wetlands were drained and turned into the Everglades Agricultural Area (EAA). Large basins called water conservation areas store water drained from the EAA. Floodgates hold or release water as needed. The dream of miles of farmland had been realized. Yet the crops would not grow. They suffered from "muck sickness." Planners overlooked the fact that Everglades plants grow in nutrient-poor conditions. The black peat soil looked fertile but lacked nutrients needed for healthy crops. Farmers added chemical fertilizers heavy in phosphates to make the crops lush and green.

The EAA cut off the lifeblood of the Everglades. The wet and dry seasons that regulated life in the Everglades no longer worked. Seasonal water flows now conformed to agricultural seasons—damaging life in the Everglades. Water now reaches the Everglades at the wrong time, in the wrong amount, and charged with phos-

New green sprouts in the Everglades Agricultural Area, while in the background smoke billows from a sugar processing plant. The rich black color of Everglades soil led early farmers to expect the soil to be fertile. In reality it lacks nutrients essential to agricultural crops and must be heavily fertilized.

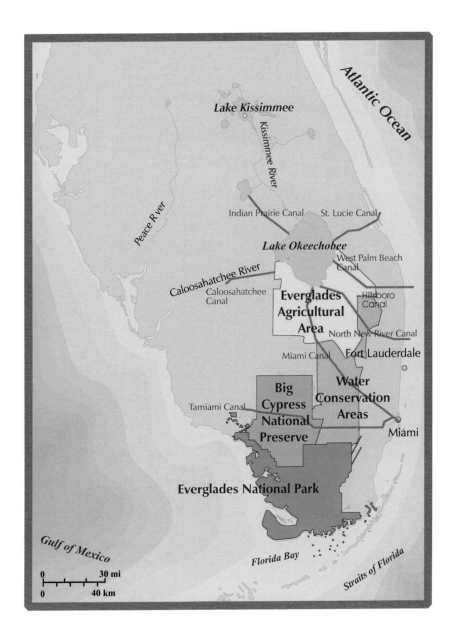

phorus from the chemical fertilizers. Some of the plants and animals in the Everglades cannot survive in this nutrient-rich water. Cattails, however, thrive on it. Cattails are a natural part of the Everglades, but before the EAA, they grew only in small, high-nutrient areas such as those around gator holes. Ted Levin, in his book on the Everglades, writes:

"The phosphorous infusion at first caused sawgrass to grow rapidly and abnormally large; then it died and gave way to cattails (*Typhus* species), which usurp fifty acres of sawgrass a day. Today more than fifty thousand acres of cattails have spread across the water conservation areas, filling in portions of the central Everglades, crowding out willow and bay, excluding fish. Wading birds

Sugar cane fields are burned before harvest to clear dead leaves and other plant trash in order to increase the speed and efficiency of harvest. Sugar is made from sugar cane or sugar beets, but more than 75 percent of the world's sugar comes from cane. With a yield ranging from 13 U.S. tons (approximately 12 metric tons) to 17 U.S. tons (15.5 metric tons), sugar is Florida's most valuable field crop. In overall agricultural economy it ranks third behind greenhouse plants and citrus. The average U.S. per capita consumption of sugar is more than 61 pounds (27.6 kg) of refined sugar. In addition, Americans consume 78 pounds (35.4 kg) of corn-based sweeteners and 1.3 pounds (.6 kg) of honey and syrups.

have no place to feed, no place to land. The composition of algal species that make up periphyton has changed. Dissolved oxygen has decreased, crippling delicate food webs."

Getting the proper nutrients to the fields is not the only problem facing the EAA. When the peat soil dries out it shrinks, oxidizes, and blows away. The peat originally averaged about 12 feet deep—now most

areas are less than half of that. According to a University of Florida study, by 2050 more than half of the EAA will have less than eight inches of soil. Sugar cane growers have devised ways to make their plants grow on less soil, but plants cannot grow on bare limestone. When the soil goes away, so will agriculture in the EAA. Then the cane growers will sell their depleted acreage to developers and move their sugar cane farms to the Caribbean.

Five hundred thousand acres of the EAA grow sugar cane. The media calls the sugar industry in Florida "Big Sugar." Sugar is big in terms of the amount of agricultural land it consumes, the soil subsidence (decrease) it causes, and the effect it has on water flow and phosphate levels in the Everglades. It is also big in terms of its contribution to the economy of Florida. Sugar brings jobs and money to the state. However, the "Big Sugar" label really comes from the big wealth and big political influence of the sugar producers. Too often, the sugar barons pull the strings of Florida politics.

Laws designed to make sugar growers and other farmers practice responsible farming often lose their bite by the time they become law. One such law was the Marjory Stoneman Douglas—Everglades Forever Act. Ms. Douglas, a noted Everglades advocate, felt that legislators weakened the act by agreeing to changes that favored sugar cane growers. The final version no longer fulfilled the promise to protect the Everglades. Ms. Douglas demanded that legislators remove her name from the act.

Florida Bay

Water slides south from the Everglades into Florida Bay, bringing with it all the ills of dysfunctional water quality, quantity, and timing. Florida Bay is a more than 850-square-mile (2200 square kilometers) estuary off the southern tip of Florida. Seven hundred square miles (1813 square kilometers) of Florida Bay are now included in Everglades National Park. In the early 1900s the bay was a paradise for marine, estuarine, and terrestrial wildlife. Its clear waters, among the most productive in the world, were nursery to more than 60 species of fish—22 of commercial importance. Countless birds bred on its mangrove islands to take advantage of the abundant seafood.

Then in 1912, Henry Flagler built a railroad that jumped from key to key carrying goods and people from the Florida mainland to Key West. It was blown apart by a hurricane in 1935, but by 1938 the remnants had been rebuilt as a highway, once again linking Key West with the mainland.

The roadbed restricted water flow and started a chain reaction that was accelerated by declining water quality from the Everglades. Here is what happened. The reduced mixing and flushing of water increased salinity to twice that of seawater. The high salt content stressed fish and promoted the growth of slime mold. The mold killed the turtle grass that covered 80 percent of the bay and provided feeding and breeding grounds for countless creatures. The decaying seagrass produced algae blooms that made the water murky and blocked sunlight, which killed more seagrass. Fish died. Birds could not find food. And the magnificent coral reef tract that covered more than 200 miles felt the effects of changing temperatures, salinity, sediment, and algae blooms, and it began to die.

By the 1980s the bay was in desperate condition. Commercial and recreational fishing were dying with the bay. Then in the 1990s an event as simple as several years of high rainfall brought fresh water to the

I Live in the Glades

Roseate Spoonbill

The roseate spoonbill (*Platalea ajaja*) feeds by sweeping its long, flat, spoon-shaped bill from side to side to strain and capture small fish, insects, and crustaceans. The spoonbill ranges from 28 to 34 inches tall (71 to 86 cm) and has a wingspan of 47 to 51 inches (47 to 51 cm).

bay and allowed it to make a partial recovery. But rainfall is unreliable. The bay needs a committed source of fresh water, but it receives only 10 percent of the water that once flowed into it from the Everglades.

Florida needs agriculture, industry, and tourism, all of which have contributed to the degradation of the Everglades. People some-

times think in terms of "should we save an alligator or save a job?" This kind of thinking is a misrepresentation of the real problem. Florida's agriculture, industry, tourism, and lifestyle all depend on a healthy environment and a stable water supply. Marjory Stoneman Douglas wrote:

"It's curious that the ignorance about the

The Tamiami Canal follows the east-west route of the Tamiami Trail (Highway 49). Water entering it from north-south canals is regulated by giant water control gates and pumps.

Everglades has persisted all these years. I suppose it's partly because Florida gets so many new residents. . . . We've got to have evaporation from the Everglades so we'll have rainfall. We need to be constantly on alert against any threat to the Kissimmee-Okeechobee-Everglades basin. It's the central support of our south Florida existence—the drinking water, all our water, all our rainfall. If the flow stops, it would mean the destruction of south Florida."

Individuals, farmers, politicians, and corporations have contributed to the plight of the Everglades. It will take action, sacrifice, and compromise by all parties involved to make the ecosystem healthy again. It will take a commitment by future generations to restore, then respect and cherish, a balanced, beautiful, and functional planet.

Chapter 6

Can We Fix the Everglades?
It's All About Working Together

I think the environment should be put in the category of our national security. Defense of our resources is just as important as defense abroad. Otherwise what is there to defend?
—Robert Redford, Yosemite National Park dedication, 1985

During a drying-out period the soil of this cypress swamp sprouts a thick cover of fresh green plants. Wetlands go through periods varying from submerged to saturated to dry. The hydropattern of a wetland refers to the depth of water, duration of inundation, and the timing and distribution of freshwater flow. The hydropattern determines the type of plants and animals that live in a wetland.

We cannot restore the Everglades ecosystem to the way it was 200, 100, or even 50 years ago. It is too late for that. But humankind is an ingenious species. The same ingenuity that learned to dig canals, build giant pumps, drain wetlands, and build skyscrapers can repair some of the damage and make the ecosystem function again.

A healthy ecosystem regulates itself. There are, however, no controls on human technology. Technology has destroyed the balance in the Everglades. Now, we are faced with the job of making it right again. We must regulate ourselves. Several plans to help the Everglades, such as the national 1972 Clean Water Act and the 1994 Everglades Forever Act, have been marred by confusion, different interpretations, and political haggling. They turned into plans to manage the water to suit human desires. The current plan, the Comprehensive Everglades Restoration Plan (CERP), recognizes that the only effective way to protect the water supply is to promote a healthy ecosystem.

What is CERP?

CERP, approved in 2000, is the largest restoration plan ever undertaken on Earth. The massive plan includes more than 50 projects in 16 counties covering an 18,000-square-mile area. Federal and state government agencies, professional groups, environmental groups, civic organizations, and scientists from many disciplines are working together toward a common goal. CERP coordinators expect the plan to take at least 35 years to complete. The cost, originally estimated at eight billion dollars, is now expected to top 12 billion.

According to the official website, CERP plans to improve or restore water flows that have changed tremendously over the past century. Canals currently dump 1.7 billion gallons (6.4 billion liters) of fresh water a day

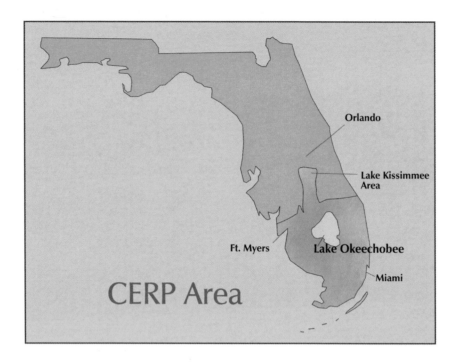

CERP Area

into Atlantic Ocean and Gulf of Mexico estuaries. The plan calls for capturing and storing as much as possible of that water. CERP plans to store the water in reservoirs, manmade wetlands, and the aquifer. In theory, the stored water can be directed to the wetlands of south Florida as needed. The stored water will also help supply urban and agricultural needs and prevent flooding. In addition, CERP will restore some drained lands to natural wetland conditions.

It is a beautiful plan. It offers hope to a vital but ailing ecosystem. It is also a plan with flaws. For instance, special interest groups are already lobbying to protect their turf. Everyone wants someone else to make the big sacrifices. Growers, developers, and residents want to protect their water supply, while environmentalists focus on getting the water right for the wildlife. Jim Livingstone, a Miami-Dade County municipal employee, points out, "The Army Corps of Engineers,

the South Florida Water Management District, the National Park Service, and the municipal water companies are all in charge of the same water and all have different goals. Plus, no one wants a tax or rate hike to pay for what needs to be done."

Having participants with different viewpoints is good. Argument and give-and-take promote compromise and balance. Saving the Everglades is going to take a lot of compromise.

Funding is another problem. The plan spans many years and costs a lot of money. Money allocated by legislators today may not actually be available when it is needed next year or ten years from now. Already, federal funds promised by former administrations have not been made available. The federal government's commitment may be boosted by the passage of the Water Resources Development Act of 2007 (WRDA). The act authourizes Army Corp of

How Much Water Do You Use?

Florida uses more water per capita than any other state except California. The 18 million people living in Florida average more than 470 gallons (1780 liters) per person per day. That is about eight billion gallons (more than 30 billion liters) of water per day. About half goes for agricultural use. Almost a third is municipal use, and about half of that goes to water lawns and gardens. In Florida severe droughts of 2006 and 2007 pointed out the need to conserve water.

What can you do? Take shorter showers. Do not let the water run while you brush your teeth. Turn off the sprinklers. Replace all or some of your grass with native ground covers, and water your remaining grass only when it wilts. When you must water, do so before the sun comes up to lose less to evaporation. Plan landscaping around native plants that are adapted to dry periods. Turn parts of your yard into natural habitat for birds, squirrels, rabbits, lizards, and other small wildlife. Not only are they fun to watch, but they will eat many of your plant pests. Set a good example and talk to people about conservation.

Engineers projects and is expected to channel two billion dollars into Florida projects, with Everglades restoration being a primary recipient.

Limited scientific knowledge is also a concern for CERP planners. The plan will use methods that have not been thoroughly tested. Scientists are not sure precisely what the results of some of their actions will be—which was also the case in the past. Good

Strangler Fig

The ficus (*Ficus aurea*), a common tree in the Everglades, is often called the strangler fig because of its unusual growing habits. Birds eat the fruit of this tree and their droppings containing seeds often lodge high in the branches of another tree. The seeds sprout there and grow toward the ground grasping the host tree in a tight hug of roots as they make their way to the ground. The tree is an epiphyte because it takes nothing from the host tree; however, unlike most epiphytes, its strangle hold will eventually kill its host. Sometimes the ficus roots completely envelop the trunk of the host, and its thick canopy robs the host of sunlight.

One photograph above shows large ficus roots tightening around a host. Another shows a young ficus growing low on a cypress. The third has completely encased a cabbage palm—palm fronds mingled with ficus branches can be seen at the top.

intentions fueled by inadequate scientific understanding of natural systems caused many of the problems the ecosystem is facing today. Straightening rivers, walling off a great lake, and networking canals across a vast wetland are all projects that were supposed to improve the land. These projects seemed, at least to some, to be good solutions to difficult problems. No one understood how disastrous the long-term results would be until it was too late. Those plans, however, were designed to benefit humans and the possible effects on the ecosystem were not considered.

CERP is supposed to benefit the Everglades ecosystem while still providing for human needs. Therefore, scientists are studying the possible long-term ecological effects of each project. Often, though, nature is unpredictable. CERP scientists and engineers will study results as the project progresses, and change techniques if they are not getting the results they wanted. Saving the Everglades calls for bold approaches and new technologies, but planners must proceed with caution. They must also continuously analyze success or failure and monitor unexpected side effects.

Putting the water right

To put the Everglades right, the water must come in the wet season and dry up in the dry season. That hydrology created the ecosystem. The water needs of the wild Everglades are often inconvenient and conflict with those of agriculture and cities. Managing the water supply for millions of acres of land with complex and conflicting needs is a large responsibility. In the past, the wild areas have come up short, but hydrologists hope that the new plan will provide for all needs.

Excess water is currently stored in Lake Okeechobee and a few water conservation areas. When there is too much water, canals dump it into Atlantic Ocean and Gulf of Mexico estuaries. An estuary is a delicately balanced mix of fresh and salt water. Too much fresh water damages the estuaries and threatens marine life, while the lower Everglades is starved for water. Too little water going to an estuary allows the water to become too salty, which also damages marine life. CERP plans to control flow patterns to both the estuaries and the freshwater wetlands with the following water conservation and storage methods:

- Aquifer Storage and Recovery (ASR)—deep wells into the aquifer. As much as 1.6 billion gallons a day may be pumped into these storage wells.
- Surface Water Storage Reservoirs. The reservoirs will cover more than 180,000 acres and will store 1.5 million acre-feet of water.
- Stormwater Treatment Areas. Approximately 35,600 acres of manmade wetlands will treat runoff water before it goes to the natural areas.
- Wastewater Reuse. Two wastewater treatment plants will clean 220 million gallons of wastewater a day for discharge into wetlands.
- Seepage Management. Millions of gallons of water are lost to seepage underground or through levees. Seepage barriers will reduce this loss.

Each of these conservation methods has some problems. For example, silt and chemical build-up can be a problem in reservoirs. The cleaned-up water will be released into the Everglades, but mimicking natural water flows may prove to be tricky. How much is enough? Too much water can be as bad as too little. Too much makes feeding difficult for wading birds and it can drown tree islands. Tree islands support 50 percent of the plant and animal life of the Everglades.

The ASRs are a major area of uncertainty. The ASR plan calls for more than 300 wells drilled 1000 feet into the brackish water of the deep aquifer. Excess surface water will be pumped into the aquifer. The difference in density between the fresh water and the brackish water should cause the freshwater to form a bubble. Large pumps can then bring freshwater back to the surface as needed.

These deep storage wells are not new technology, but have never been tested on such a large scale. There are many unanswered questions about how successful

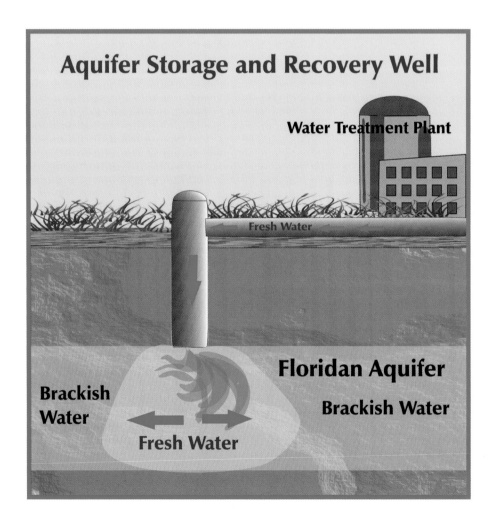

they will be. Questions that hydrologists and geologists are struggling with include the following:

- What effect will the additional water have on the existing underground water system?
- Could the additional pressure cause cracks in the aquifer rock?
- How will the water quality change, and what effect will the changes have on the environment and the health of the people, plants, and animals living in it?
- How much of the stored water can be recovered?

Some scientists are concerned that ASR storage may be another solution that sounds good, but only because we do not understand the long-term results.

Golden Gate Estates— wasteland to wetland

Everyone wants to retire in sunny Florida— or so it seemed in the 1950s when Gulf American Corporation, a real estate development company, bought 173 square miles (448 square kilometers) in and around Big Cypress Swamp. The developer sold small parcels of the American dream sight-unseen to thousands of buyers. Golden Gate Estates was advertised as "the world's largest subdivision."

The growl of heavy equipment rattles through a section of Prairie Canal in Picayune National Forest (formerly Southern Golden Gate Estates). It looks like just another construction site eating up more of the Everglades, but the digging and scraping are the first steps in restoring the natural wetland elevations and water conditions.

I Live in the Glades

Tree Snails

Liguus tree snails (*Liguus fasciatus*), the little gems of the Everglades, were once common in Everglades hardwood hammocks. These colorful two- to three inch (five- to seven-centimeter) tree snails come in almost sixty variations of pattern and color. They range from solid brown or white to bright stripes or wild color flares in pink, yellow, and green. During the wet summer months they slither along tropical tree trunks dining on fungus and lichens. As the dry winter season approaches the snails make their way to the ground and bury a clutch of eggs at the base of the tree. The adult snail then returns to the tree where it sticks itself to the trunk and estivates until the spring rains return. Estivation is a dormant stage similar to hibernation. The beautiful liguus is now rare due to loss of habitat, shell collecting, spraying for mosquitoes, and drowning of eggs by disruption of natural water flow patterns.

Gulf American built roads and dug canals to drain the wetland. Buyers built homes in Northern Golden Gate Estates, then found that in spite of the drainage canals the low-lying land still flooded in the rainy season. Newer residents built their homes on mounds of earth to raise them above flood levels. It helped some—by pushing more floodwater into their neighbor's yards.

Southern Golden Gate Estates (SGGE) stayed nearly vacant, but the canals and roads changed the ecology of the area. CERP plans to turn the land back into productive wetland. The state bought 85 square miles (220 square kilometers) of SGGE from thousands of owners scattered around the world. Locating the owners and buying the land was an amazing feat, and it was just the beginning.

Before restoration could begin, scientists had to have a baseline—a record of what the area was like when they started. Biologists with the Conservancy of Southwest Florida identified five major habitats within SGGE. They sampled small mammals, fish, reptiles, amphibians, and insects, and analyzed the species composition and abundance of these wildlife related to the habitats. For example, they found 39 species of ants! They also identified species as native or exotic. Twelve of the ant species are not native to the area. Ants respond quickly to environmental change and therefore are good indicators of restoration effects. As the restoration progresses, they will continue to monitor populations if funding is available.

Hydrologists are attempting to recreate the wetland by plugging canals and grading roads to eliminate ditches and berms that change the flow of water. If the restoration is successful, native species should become more

The canals of the former SGGE are filled in sections, giving them a dotted-line look. There is not enough fill available to completely fill the canals, but the plugs will stop the water from draining into the sea. According to Dr. Schmid, if fill becomes available the remaining sections will be filled later to return the area to as much of a natural state as possible. In the meantime, he noted, alligators and other wildlife are making themselves at home in the unfilled sections.

A road near Prairie Canal has been graded and the berms on the sides of the road leveled so that the area can return to natural conditions.

stable and theoretically exotics should decline. For example, Brazilian pepper thrives on the dry berms created by road grading, but should disappear when the land becomes wetland again. However, other exotic species could successfully compete with native species and become established. Biologists must continue to be vigilant in order for the restoration to be successful.

Lake Okeechobee

Lake Okeechobee is a critical part of the greater Everglades watershed. In the summer wet season, water that once made its way slowly through wetlands to Lake Okeechobee is now channeled directly to the lake by drainage ditches and canals. This causes the watershed to dry up and the lake to be too deep. The water is then dumped into the Caloosahatchee and St. Lucie estuaries. This changes the estuaries and causes algae blooms and marine life die-offs. In contrast, in the winter dry season, the lake drops unnaturally low. There is not enough water to provide for human needs and certainly not enough to provide for the water needs of the Everglades. Plans to restore the lake include wetland water storage and stormwater treatment areas both above and below the lake. This will help to return the more natural flow patterns in and out of the lake. The damage caused by extreme high or low levels in the lake should improve.

The Audubon Society estimates that an additional 1.2 million acre feet of water-storage area is needed north of the lake and

Everglades Sheet Flow Patterns

Historical

Current

Proposed

one million acre feet is needed south of the lake. One of the biggest obstacles the project faces is buying enough land to provide the additional storage.

Another big problem for Lake Okeechobee is the amount of phosphorus the water brings into the lake. Historically, the water was cleansed as it passed through the wetlands. Now it gushes directly into the lake loaded with phosphorus and other pollutants. The lake receives an average inflow of 500 to 600 tons of phosphorus a year. The CERP goal is 105 tons per year. CERP will work with property owners to reduce the amount of phosphorus coming from their land. They will also treat phosphorus-laden water before it reaches the lake.

Unfortunately, decomposing plants and algae on the lake bottom contain huge amounts of phosphorus. Even if inflow goals are met, it will take decades for the phosphorus pollution already in the lake to reach acceptable levels. Restoration scientists are experimenting with Periphyton-based Stormwater Treatment Areas (PSTA) to reduce phosphorus levels. The marl layer produced by periphyton covers decomposing vegetation and forms a shield that seals the phosphorus-rich layer to the lake bottom so that it cannot mix with the water.

Lake Okeechobee is world famous for its fishing and wildlife. However, the pollution in the lake has had a disastrous effect on wildlife. Dr. Paul Gray reports in an Audubon publication:
"As a result of exotic species invasions, pollution, and unseasonably high and low water, Lake Okeechobee's wildlife resources have suffered greatly. Snail Kites have not nested successfully on the lake for a decade. Large-scale wading bird nesting and foraging only occurs erratically. Loss of some 60 square miles of submerged plants during recent high water apparently has decimated the largemouthed bass fishery. Similarly, black crappie have not successfully reproduced in two years. Land use changes in the watershed are reducing Florida's endemic prairie bird fauna, including Caracaras, Florida Grasshopper Sparrows and Florida Sandhill Cranes."

Kissimmee River — returning the meander

Turning the Kissimmee River into a dead canal and draining the surrounding wetland may be one of the most disastrous environmental projects in history. Public outrage was voiced long before its completion in 1971. People wanted the river to meander again. Marjory Stoneman Douglas wrote, "Congress voted $60,000 for the engineers to study this. Of course, they love to study it. They'd keep on studying it until the cows came home. Then they'd ask for more money for another study." The study eventually determined that the river could be fixed, but progress has been slow. However, when completed it will be the largest river restoration project in the history of the Earth.

Audubon of Florida has praised the project for its scientific approach and evaluation of each phase of the project. A large-scale model of the river system was constructed at the University of California, Berkeley. Scientists use the model to better understand how their actions will affect flow, sediment, and erosion.

Finally, the meander is returning. Sections of Canal 38, the project that changed the Kissimmee River from a wildlife paradise to a polluted ditch, have been filled and the river allowed to
meander across the landscape. When the project is complete more than 40 miles of the river
will slither through a vast wetland once again.

Engineers cannot put the river back just as it was, but they hope to make it function as a wetland again and provide a more hospitable home for wildlife. Once finished, 43 miles (70 km) of river channel will again meander through central Florida to Lake Okeechobee, and 27,000 acres of wetland will clean the water on its way to the lake. This wetland will feed Lake Okeechobee and should help control extremes in water levels.

The Kissimmee project was begun before CERP was conceived, but its completion is vital to the overall goals of CERP. As of 2007, only seven and a half miles of the canal have been filled; however the project is back on track with an estimated completion date between 2010 and 2012. According to Dr. Gray:

"Much of the delay has been due to difficulty in acquiring the necessary land, however, 99.8 percent of the land needed for restoration has been purchased, and back-filling of the northern end of the canal is in progress. A critical land purchase has made it possible to proceed with restoration of the lower part of the river. There are myriad side projects such as raising Hwy 98 (done) and the railroad bridge (not done), improving a structure on the Istokpoga Canal (in progress), taking out ditches in the flood-plain (mostly done), etc., that are part of the project."

The most exciting thing about the Kissimmee project is that it clearly shows that careful, scientifically planned restoration of the physical features of a wetland can result in the return of natural plant and wildlife populations. Wetland species, from fish and birds to invertebrates, are rapidly repopulating restored areas of the Kissimmee wetland—proof that human ingenuity can work with nature to recreate a functioning environment.

It is true that CERP has flaws, questions, uncertainties, and disagreements; even so, it is a beautiful plan. It is the only plan comprehensive enough to have a chance of saving the Everglades. But it cannot stand alone. The entire community must support the effort by making compromises and living in an environmentally responsible way. Individuals, businesses, builders, and farmers are awakening to the fact that everyone wins if we use resources in a sustainable way.

Conscientious development

Housing for humans is a necessary part of the environment. Nevertheless, residential areas should have as little impact as possible on the environment. In the past, many south Florida builders showed little concern for the environment, but that is changing. Some forward-looking developers are building a healthy environment into their community plans.

Bonita Bay Group, for example, un-derstands that creating communities in harmony with nature enhances the lifestyles of its residents. Bonita Bay Group communities, between Ft. Myers and Naples, blend nature and development as seamlessly as possible by preserving existing natural and archaeological features. In addition, the developer restores natural flowways and wildlife corridors. The use of native plants encourages water conservation and allows natural habitat and landscaping to merge. Bonita Bay provides environmental education and community guidelines to aid residents in applying the same standards to their yards. Bonita Bay Group golf courses meet strict Audubon Cooperative Sanctuary Program for Golf Courses (ACSP) certification standards.

Responsible farming

Much of the overload of phosphorus and other chemicals in the Everglades comes from farm runoff. Some farmers are using innovative methods to reduce the amount of pollutants that leave their property. Farmers can reduce erosion and polluted runoff from their land by

- Building closed-loop irrigation systems that reuse water rather than allowing it to drain off the farm;
- Leveling fields so that water spreads evenly over them and does not puddle, run off, or cause soil erosion;
- Building low banks or berms along ditches and canal banks to keep the water in the fields rather than

Bonita Bay Group's 2,532-acre Brooks community was designed to blend the needs of the environment and human housing. Land that had been filled and drained for grazing cattle was redesigned to approximate the historical typography. An interlocking system of marshes, streams, and lakes now connects with the original wetlands and flowways. The result has relieved flooding, brought wildlife back, and created a beautiful environment for homes.

Computerized Roadkill

Highways bring sudden death to hundreds of wild animals every year. Highways also break habitat into small, unconnected areas, sometimes separating animals from traditional breeding or feeding places. Large mammals such as panthers and black bears need a large territory to roam over and often must cross roads in their travels. Roads are a necessary part of human life, but when they form barriers, animals suffer from lack of genetic diversity, food shortages, or the risk of becoming roadkill.

Highway planners are concerned about the needs of wildlife, but in the past have not clearly understood what areas were most sensitive or what could be done about it. An innovative computer research team at the University of Florida's Landscape Ecology Program designed a computer program to give the Department of Transportation the information it needs. The group developed a Geographic Information System (GIS) that analyzes information on hydrology, land use, species distribution, and existing roads and greenways. Using information from transportation and wildlife experts, the system can identify chronic roadkill sites, biodiversity hot spots, animal corridors, and rare habitat types. Highway engineers can use the information to design roads to meet the needs of both humans and wildlife. They can also find the most serious problem areas on existing roads and schedule them for immediate attention.

I Live In the Glades

Yellow-crowned Night-heron

The nocturnal yellow-crowned night-heron (*Nyctanassa violacoa*) stalks its prey or stands still at the waters edge waiting in ambush. It eats crustaceans, mollusks, frogs, aquatic insects, and small fish. Adults stand 22 to 28 inches tall (60 to 70 cm).

running into the canal;

- Using sumps and traps to catch sediment before it drains away from the farm, then returning the sediment to the fields;

- Planting cover crops on fields not in use and along canal banks to hold the soil.

Florida Water Management district offices assist farmers by testing new conservation methods, providing demonstrations, and advising individual farmers on the best technology for their farms.

And what about the rest of us?

Businesses, farmers, industries, and institutions are learning to dispose of their wastes more responsibly, manage agricultural and parking lot runoff, reduce use of pesticides, and use environmentally friendly landscaping. That brings it down to you and me. As individuals we are the most powerful players in the game.

We can support conservation by buying from responsible producers. Stay aware of environmental improvements in industry and agriculture. Then let merchants know that you prefer products from growers and manufacturers who attempt to limit their negative effect on the earth. Do you golf? Golf courses destroy natural habitat, and runoff from fairways dumps phosphates and nitrogen into nearby waterways. Enjoy your golf, but protect the environment. Play on Audubon-certified courses or ask club managers what their course is doing to minimize its impact on the ecology. Vote. Listen to what the candidates say about the environment and look up their voting record to see if they practice what they preach. A good website for keeping up with your congressional representatives is www.govtrack.us. Make noise. Talk to people about environmental stewardship.

Be personally conservative. Small changes are like drops in a bucket—they will eventually fill the bucket. In other words, you can make a big difference a little bit at a time. Think about the way you live. When you turn the faucet on, think what you can do to use a little less water. Look for ways to produce a little less garbage. For example, do not use two paper towels when one will do. Avoid buying over-packaged products. You cannot put your green beans in your pocket, but you can buy the ones you drop into a plastic bag rather than the ones that are placed on a Styrofoam tray then wrapped in plastic. You can take it one step further by taking your own reusable string bags to the store with you. Always recycle any plastic bags you do have to use.

Be vigilant. Marjory Stoneman Douglas said, "The most unhappy thing about conservation is that it is never permanent. If we save a priceless woodland today, it is threatened from another quarter tomorrow." We can only make conservation permanent by staying alert to threats."

Chapter 7
Heroes and Protected Lands
The Fight to Save the Special Places

Never doubt that a small group of thoughtful, committed citizens
can change the world; indeed, it is the only thing that ever has. —Margaret Mead

A tourist walkway rises above the landscape and curves toward a tower viewing platform located near the tram and bike trail at Shark Valley in Everglades National Park. For national and state parks, meeting commitments to make the parks accessible to the public while still protecting sensitive ecosystems is challenging. This tower and walkway is designed to provide maximum viewing with minimum impact on the surrounding area.

ou can make a difference. Persistent, passionate, and persuasive individuals have focused international attention on the abuse of the Everglades. Floridians have confronted the legislature, formed groups, organized protests, filed lawsuits, and talked and talked to anyone who would listen and many who would not. They have faced indifference and sometimes hostility to bring attention to the need to protect the ecosystem. Finally, the biggest restoration project on earth is under way. It would not have happened without the efforts of concerned citizens.

George Bird Grinnell founded the National Audubon Society to protect the slaughter of birds for their plumes. Marjory Stoneman Douglas organized the Friends of the Everglades and helped block the building of a jetport in a sensitive area of the wetland. Others have taken a different route and used their art to focus attention on the Everglades. Archie Carr, Peter Matthiesson, Ted Levin, Carl Hiassen, and, of course, Marjory Stoneman Douglas have written about the Everglades with sensitivity, wit, and wisdom. Visual artists, including Winslow Homer and John James Audubon, have preserved the colors, wildlife, and spirit of the ecosystem in oils and watercolor. Clyde Butcher, James Valentine, and Jeff Ripple are among the talented photographers who have captured the ever-changing moods of the Everglades. People cannot care about something they do not know. These works of art introduce people to the Everglades.

Other individuals contribute as much as their skills and time allow. For example, former football coach and NFL player "Sanibel Sam" Bailey says, "Something needs to be done about Lake Okeechobee. They are dumping all that water into the Caloosahatchee and hitting us broadside with it. It is killing our bay. They are doing the same thing on the other side of the state with the St. Lucie." Now in his eight-

White-tail Deer

The white-tail deer (*Odocoileus virginianus*), a common but secretive resident of the Everglades, is an important food source for the endangered Florida panther. It is also the most important big game mammal in North America. The average amount spent by hunters on guns, ammunition, other hunting equipment, deer hunting licenses, food, and travel expenses is about $1,500 for each deer harvested. Hunting licenses help fund wildlife management.

White-tail deer in Florida tend to be smaller than those in more northern climates. Smaller still is the endangered Key deer, a subspecies of the white-tail deer that lives only in the Florida Keys. In northern states a white-tail buck (male deer) may weigh 300 pounds or more (136 kg), while south Florida bucks weigh about 125 pounds (56 kg). The typical Florida Key deer weighs in at a mere 80 pounds (39 kg).

Male deer sport magnificent antlers. The antlers are not true horns; they are decidous outgrowths on bony plates on the skull. Decidous means they fall off every year and regrow. Antlers are important in courtship and mating. The antlers are at their peak size in time for rut (breeding season) and fall off when it is over. The time of year for rut varies from place to place. In the north deer usually rut in the fall and fawns are born in spring or early summer. Florida deer, however, have evolved to take advantage of the local climate and in south Florida rut is usually timed so that the deer give birth in the dry winter months.

ies, Bailey intends to do something about it. In addition to helping his brother run their century-old business, Bailey's Store, he spends approximately 20 hours a week in meetings and correspondence attempting to stop the inflow of fresh water into the estuary around Sanibel Island.

Not everyone can devote large amounts of time, but many individuals and organizations have taken a stand to protect the Everglades. Each one is important, but a few stand out as special heroes.

Marjory Stoneman Douglas —voice of the river

Twenty-five-year-old Marjory Stoneman Douglas (1890–1998) came to south Florida in 1915 to work on her father's newspaper—the paper that would become the *Miami Herald*. She did not come expecting to fall head over heels in love with a great mucky marsh. And indeed, it was not love at first sight. Hers was the love that grows with knowledge and understanding.

Ms. Douglas began to know the Ever-

Marjory Stoneman Douglas, the grand dame of Everglades restoration, was inducted into the Women's Hall of Fame in 1986 and received the Presidential Medal of Honor from President Clinton in 1993.

glades on early morning trips with friends to a road still under construction. They stopped and cooked breakfast where the new Tamiami Trail ended. The new road was inching its way westward into the middle of the Everglades. Midway it would meet its other half crawling eastward from Naples. Ms. Douglas and her friends enjoyed breakfast watching the warm morning light slowly expose green tree islands and shimmer on golden sawgrass. One morning was special. Ms. Douglas remembers, "We looked out at a great wheel of white birds slowly drifting over the land. It was an extraordinary sight. Birds seemed to leap into the air and then swing around in a huge circle. As soon as one group landed on the ground, another would lift off and fly." They had witnessed the mating flight of the white ibis.

The subtle beauty of the Everglades entranced Ms. Douglas. More importantly, she understood the need to keep the ecosystem healthy. However, seeing the Everglades from the dry ground of a roadbed was good enough for her. She said, "To be a friend of the Everglades is not necessar-

I Live in the Glades

Brown Pelican

The brown pelican (*Pelecanus occidentalis*) almost disappeared from the southeastern United States and California in the early 1970s due to spraying of the pesticide DDT. The DDT caused the pelican's eggshells to become too thin to support the weight of the developing embryos. DDT was banned in 1972 and brown pelicans are once again a common sight in the Everglades. With a wingspan of 6 to 8.2 ft (1.83 to 2.5 m) the brown pelican, the smallest of the eight species of pelican, is still a large bird. Pelicans scoop water into the large flexible pouch on their beaks, strain out the water, and eat the remaining fish or squid. Brown pelicans, unlike other pelican species, also feed by plunge diving from high above the surface to grab an unsuspecting fish. Brown pelicans like the company of other pelicans and often travel together, flying single file low over the water's surface. Colonies nest together, usually on islands, with nests that vary from a simple scrape in the sand to a stick nest built in a low hanging tree.

ily to spend time wandering around out there. It's too buggy, too wet, too generally inhospitable for camping or hiking or the other outdoors activities … I suppose you could say the Everglades and I had the kind of friendship that doesn't depend on constant physical contact."

She began to write articles about the Glades, but her career often took her away from Florida. She always returned to her little house in Miami, and each time she saw further damage to her beloved Everglades. Her concern grew. In 1947 she wrote *The Everglades: River of Grass*. The book was an immediate success and brought public and political attention to the relentless draining of the Everglades. The same year, Everglades National Park was established. The park was the result of 25 years of advocacy by Ms. Douglas and a committee headed by Ernest Coe. In 1993 Ms. Douglas received the Presidential Medal of Freedom for her efforts to save the Everglades.

At 79, Ms. Douglas began her public speaking career. She first spoke to recruit members for her new Friends of the Everglades organization. Those first speeches were the beginning of the final phase of her long love affair with the Everglades. For more than 20 years she traveled and talked about the Everglades. Her strong opinions and a quick wit made her a popular speaker. Whether she was speaking to a women's club or the Florida Legislature, she never hesitated to say exactly what she thought. When her eyesight failed, she declared that she might not be able to see, but she could still talk. Marjory Stoneman Douglas talked about the love of her life, the Everglades, until she died in 1998 at age 108.

Ernest Coe—father of the park

Ernest Coe (1866–1951) wanted a park and made it happen. Coe, a graduate of Yale University School of Fine Arts, came to south Florida to work as a landscape architect. He lost his money in land speculations, but stayed in Florida to promote the idea of setting a portion of the Everglades aside as a park.

Marjory Stoneman Douglas described her friend Ernest as always wearing a seersucker suit frayed at the sleeves and always talking about his park. He talked, in fact, for 25 years before Congress finally established Everglades National Park in 1947. The park was both a triumph and a disappointment. He thought it should include a large section of Big Cypress Swamp north of the Tamiami Trail, but the park was established without that land. Coe foresaw that without a large area north of the road, the park would

not be able to control the water supply it needed to survive. Coe resigned from the committee in anger and never participated again. He did, however, attend President Truman's dedication of the park held in Everglades City.

Guy Bradley—martyr to the cause

Guy Bradley (1870–1906) grew up in the Everglades. He loved the wild country and the creatures it sheltered. Like most Gladesmen he made his living off the land, even occasionally taking a few birds for their plumes. Hats adorned with bird plumes were high style in the fashion centers of the world. Plumes from Everglades birds in breeding colors brought a fortune by Glades standards. The temptation was understandable. Hunters could kill a few birds to supplement a meager income and could take home wild bird dinner as well. Many plume hunters, however, carried it much farther. They wiped out whole rookeries, leaving baby birds to die and eggs to rot.

The American Ornithological Society successfully lobbied the Florida Legislature for a law to protect the birds. They hired Guy Bradley, then a Monroe County deputy, as warden to enforce the new law. Bradley

The Ernest F. Coe Visitors Center, one of five visitor centers in Everglades National Park, offers interpretive displays of park habitats. Some visitor centers have walking trails or offer boat or tram rides, and all have small gift and refreshment shops.

The Fakahatchee Strand, one of the most beautiful and diverse areas of the Everglades ecosystem, is expected to benefit significantly from filling the canals in the adjacent former Southern Golden Gate Estates. Water that traditionally reached the strand has been channeled to the sea by the canal.

took his job seriously and made many enemies among the plume hunters. He knew that his life was at risk but never hesitated in his mission.

Bradley was 35 years old when, on July 8, 1905, a plume hunter shot and killed him. He left behind a wife and two young children. Even after his death Bradley served the Everglades well. His murder brought national attention to the Everglades and the trade in plumes. His martyrdom supported bird conservation laws and helped promote the idea of setting a part of the Everglades aside as a national park.

More heroes

Arthur Marshall (1919–1985) was a dedicated conservationist who participated in practically every organization dedicated to preserving the Everglades. He studied the work of many different scientists and brought their ideas together into one big picture highlighting the interconnections of the ecosystem. He used the information to write a plan for saving the Everglades.

Marshall's close friend, Marjory Stoneman Douglas, made the initial donation to start the Arthur Marshall Foundation. Mr. Marshall died in 1985 before the foundation became a reality. His nephew **John Arthur Marshall**, a retired marine officer, picked up where he left off and started the Foundation in 1998. He still serves as its president. The Foundation differs from other Everglades organizations because it provides hands-on restoration experience to people of all ages.

By 1988 conditions in Everglades National Park were so bad that the United

Arthur Marshall

John Marshall

Volunteers Alex Avalos and John Callovi plant trees for the Arthur R. Marshall Foundation, an organization that provides hands-on restoration experiences to residents of all ages. Foundation volunteers have planted more than 80,000 wetland trees and almost 2000 pounds of cypress seeds at sites throughout the Everglades watershed.

States Department of Justice sued Florida for allowing polluted runoff from sugar cane farms to damage the ecosystem. **Judge William Hoeveler** presided over the case. Judge Hoeveler was determined to see that the state upheld its promise to clean up the Everglades. In 2003 he publicly expressed concerns over a new law that gave the sugar industry an additional ten years to meet clean water requirements. In spite of the fact that Judge Hoeveler was known as one of Florida's most fair jurists, the sugar industry successfully petitioned the court to remove him from the case.

Due to the efforts of these and other dedicated individuals and groups, Everglades cleanup is moving ahead and approximately 3 million acres of the Everglades are protected as national and state parks, preserves, and other public lands.

Everglades National Park

With 1,508,000 acres, Everglades National Park is Florida's largest park. Everglades National Park receives more than a million visitors each year—one-third of them from outside the United States.

Visitors enjoy wildlife viewing and recreational opportunities, but the park's ecological importance is global. Everglades National Park was named a UNESCO World Heritage Site in 1979, and since 1993 has been listed as a World Heritage Site in Danger. The park is also a UNESCO International Biosphere Reserve and a Ramsar Convention Wetland of International Importance.

According to Rick Cook, former Everglades National Park public relations officer,

issues relating to the quality and quantity of water are the most serious threats to the park. Events outside the park have cut the flow and quality of the water the park needs to survive. Cook feels that CERP is crucial to the survival of the park. When asked if he thought it was too late to save the park, Cook responded: "I don't think it is, but I think there will be a day when it is too late. Our scientists think it has been a very resilient system, and think some of the function can be brought back. We are not really restoring the Everglades. . . . Many of the things we are doing are sort of artificially reproducing the conditions we want."

Other national parks

Two other national parks are included in the Everglades ecosystem. **Biscayne National Park** is unique in that 95 percent of its 181,500 acres are underwater. It is a popular site for snorkeling, fishing, and other water

Snorkelers explore elkhorn coral at Biscayne National Park. National park status protects land and water from on-site development, but it cannot protect delicate coral reefs from problems that begin outside the park such as pollution or disruption of natural water flow patterns.

activities. The park also includes a stretch of mainland shoreline and a number of small islands.

Biscayne National Park also preserves the remnants of an interesting bit of Florida history. In the 1930s a shack was built on stilts in Biscayne Bay. The idea became trendy, and eventually Stiltsville, a community of fine homes and several clubs, stood like squatty storks in the bay. The Park plans to preserve the remaining buildings and convert them to park facilities.

A cluster of seven coral and sand islands 70 miles west of Key West have been preserved as **Dry Tortugas National Park**. There is no fresh water on the islands and they were once home to large numbers of sea turtles—*las tortugas* means "the turtles" in Spanish, hence the name. Dry Tortugas is best known for its bird and marine life, its tales of pirate treasure, and its history as a military outpost.

Other federal properties are also very important to the Everglades. For example, **Big Cypress National Preserve** covers 720,567 acres of lush swampland. It brings under federal protection much of the land Ernest Coe wanted included in the national park. A national preserve is much like a national park, but without the same restrictions. For example, the Seminole and Miccosukee people have permanent rights to live in and use Big Cypress. Big Cypress shelters numerous endangered and threatened species including the Florida panther.

Another significant national preserve is the **Archie Carr National Wildlife Refuge**. Archie Carr, an internationally known sea turtle expert, was the source of much of our knowledge about sea turtles. The Refuge honors Carr by setting aside a section of sea turtle nesting sites for their protection. The refuge is located just south of Melbourne.

State parks and forests

Florida has approximately 40 state parks located within the Everglades ecosystem—starting just north of Lake Okeechobee. They preserve choice environmental and historical features. **John Pennekamp Coral Reef State Park**, covering 70 nautical square miles, was the first underwater park in the United States. **John U. Lloyd Beach State Park** is popular with nesting sea turtles as well as beachcombers. An 11-square-mile island that was the first county seat of Dade County is now **Indian Key State Park**.

Fakahatchee Strand State Preserve is a particularly valuable slice of the Everglades. The linear swamp park stretches 20 miles long by five miles wide through the heart of the wild Everglades. It hosts a wide array of habitats and is home to many wildlife species, including the Florida panther, black bear, Everglades mink, and indigo snake. With 44 native orchids and 14 bromeliads, the strand has more of these plant species than any other place in the continental United States. Fakahatchee Strand water levels are expected to improve now that Prairie Canal, one of the canals that drained Southern Golden Gate Estates (SGGE), is being filled. SGGE is now part of the 70,000-acre Picayune State Forest.

Numerous other properties belonging to state and federal governments, con-

Manager Art Yerian, of Homosassa Springs Wildlife State Park, takes a few minutes out of his day to feed the new baby. The abandoned male black bear cub stayed at the park for several weeks before being sent to live at the Bush Wildlife Sanctuary in Jupiter, Florida. The wildlife park cares for injured and abandoned animals from all over the state, and when possible returns them to life in the wild. The park performs a vital function while providing visitors the opportunity to view native wildlife in a beautiful shady setting.

servancies, institutions, and environmental organizations have been set aside to preserve as much as possible of the south Florida Everglades ecosystem. The problem is that these lands cannot exist as islands. They are all part of an integrated ecosystem. If the water flow is broken or polluted they suffer. Activity in the Everglades Agricultural Area and development in Naples or Miami affect the entire ecosystem. Even so, these protected lands are very important to the survival of the Everglades. If their water needs can be met, the parks and reserves assure us that there will always be wild land for wildlife and recreation and to preserve the water source for south Florida.

Conservation usually requires government intervention. But it takes public demand to spur governments into action. Individuals working together can save the Everglades.

Career Opportunities

Humankind is facing the most challenging and exciting job of all time—the job of restoring, protecting, and maintaining Planet Earth. We thought it could absorb whatever abuse we heaped on it. Now we know that it cannot. It has become frayed, a bit tattered and worn. We have to fix it. The job calls for many skills. Hydrologist, biologist, computer specialist, doctor, lawyer, Indian chief—whatever your interests, you can be part of it.

The Everglades is all about water. Hence, hydrologists—specialists in water quality, quantity, timing, and source—play a major role in Everglades restoration. The word environment brings to mind life sciences—such as biology and ecology and the many specialties within them. However, these fields are only the beginning. Physical scientists, including geologists and chemists, must contribute understanding of the substance and forces of the earth. Environmental engineers are required to design highways, bridges, water systems, and structures that work with natural systems rather than against them. Mechanical engineers and inventors are needed to design environmentally friendly tools and equipment.

Hardware and software designers and operators are frontline soldiers in the fight to save the environment. With their skills, we can catalog, store, analyze, and share information in a way that was unheard of fifty years ago. With a few keystrokes we can virtually travel the world to learn how other places are resolving similar problems. Environmental attorneys and lawmakers build the legal system that puts the teeth in reform. Teachers, writers, and artists are the tattletales and cheerleaders who keep us all informed. Environmental reform relies on many specialties and many individuals. Let's meet a few of the individuals who are working to save the Everglades.

Dr. Jeffrey R. Schmid is an Environmental Research Manager with The Conservancy of Southwest Florida. So, what does that mean? How does Jeff Schmid spend his day? Some days he puts on waders and mucks around in the Everglades studying the communities of organisms that live there

Dr. Jeff Schmid examines the contents of a small mammal trap used to sample populations in the Southern Golden Gate Estates restoration area.

or he sloshes through the estuaries mapping habitat types. He spends other days in front of a computer analyzing research data, filing reports, and writing papers for publication. He is also well known as a sea turtle specialist. In the evenings, he teaches college-level courses to help other people understand how the environment relates to life in Florida.

Jeff's wife, **Jill Schmid**, is also a biologist. At Rookery Bay National Estuarine Research Reserve, she combines her interest in sea turtles with her GIS (Geographical Informational System) skills to produce maps of natural and cultural resources within the Reserve. GIS is a computer system for capturing, managing, analyzing, and geographically displaying data. GIS enables Jill to see patterns emerge by studying the distribution of features on a map. Jill monitors sea turtle nesting, conducts seagrass surveys, manages the GIS database, and trains staff on using GIS, global positioning system (GPS) equipment, and other environmental software.

Jill Schmid holds a melaleuca sapling she pulled up in the SGGE restoration area.

Jeanette Hobbs is employed by a conservation organization. She says, "I guess you would describe my job as 'restoration ecologist.'" Jeanette assists landholders with restoration projects. Many of those landholders are state and federal agencies lacking the staff to undertake the myriad details of restoration projects. That is where Jeanette comes in. She secures the funding and helps design a project that meets the landholder's goals. Goals may include habitat restoration or benefit a particular endangered species. Jeanette obtains the permits, collects and manages the money, hires contractors, and oversees the project. When the project is done, she writes reports on the restoration process and files periodic follow-up reports. Jeanette is also a talented nature photographer and contributed some beautiful images to this book.

Jeanette Hobbs checks a water sample on a project site.

Kim Fikoski, Senior Environmental Affairs Manager for Bonita Bay Group, has the formidable task of managing all of a large developer's required permits for building in environmentally sensitive areas. She works with state, federal, and local agencies to help Bonita Bay build environmentally friendly residential communities. Kim makes sure the company stays on track to adhere to sound ecological practices and produce community environments that enhance the lifestyles of both humans and wildlife.

Patrick Ramsey is a seasonal park ranger at Everglades National Park. Seasonal rangers move from park to park to help boost the staff during busy times. Ranger Pat works at the Grand Canyon in the summer and at parks with winter seasons, such as Everglades National Park, in the winter. Most rangers, however, work year-round in the same park. Ranger duties include law enforcement, trail maintenance, education and outreach, and helping visitors enjoy the park experience. Ranger Pat says, "To really experience the park you have to open your mind and listen to what it is telling you."

Parks also offer a wide range of employment opportunities in areas including biology, hydrology, administration, and, through concessionaires, gift shop and food service management.

Where are the jobs? Many environmental jobs are with state and federal agencies and landholders. Private organizations such as Audubon, World Wildlife Fund, nature conservancies, private refuges, parks, and preserves also offer employ-

ment opportunities. More and more private enterprises are recognizing the necessity to conduct their business in an environmentally friendly way and are creating jobs for people to help them understand environmental needs.

What are the requirements? An interest in environmental stewardship is the primary requirement, because job opportunities are so varied. Some positions require a doctorate degree or other specialized education, but there are opportunities available on many levels. Some government agencies and private organizations offer scholarships or internships. For example, The Arthur Marshall Foundation offers a ten-week paid internship to college and graduate school students. The internship focuses on Everglades ecology and restoration. For more information visit their website at www.artmarshall.org. There are also many opportunities for volunteers of all ages and skills.

Restoring, preserving, and protecting the Everglades and other natural areas is a huge responsibility and requires teamwork by the global community. But together we have the skills, ingenuity, and determination to make it happen.

Notes

Chapter 1
p. 9 Carr, Archie, and the Editors of Time-Life Books, *The Everglades,* New York: Time-Life Books, 1973, p. 108

p. 13 Carr, *The Everglades,* p. 140

Chapter 2
p. 17 Larry Ogren, Retired, Endangered Species Specialist, National Marine Fisheries Service, interview with author, January 2006.

p. 27 Larry Ogren, January 2006

Chapter 3
p. 30 What Killed the Dinosaurs: The Great Mystery, DinoBuzz, website of The University of California, Berkeley website: http://www.ucmp.berkeley.edu/diapsids/dinobuzz.html

p. 30 Virginia Morell, *The Sixth Extinction,* National Geographic, February 1999

p. 30 The Wood Stork: Indicator of an Endangered Everglades, Everglades National Park website, http://www.nps.gov/ever/current/wdstork2.htm

p. 35 Stuart L. Pimm, *The World According to Pimm,* New York: McGraw Hill, 2001. p.1

p. 38 Sharon Rauch, *Putting Down Roots: Exotics in the Everglades,* "The Book of the Everglades," Susan Cerulean, p. 143, Milkweed Editions, 2002, Minneapolis, Minnesota

Chapter 4
p. 44 Hernando D'Escalante Fontaneda, *Fontaneda's Memoir,* translated by Buckingham Smith 1854, edited by Jerry Wilkinson, Keys, http://keys history.org/Fontenada.html, Historeum, Historical Preservation Society of the Upper Keys, http://keyshistory.org/index.html

p. 48 Storter, p. 13

p. 50 Simmons, p 10

p. 50 Simmons, p 12

p. 50 Tebeau, Charlton W., *Man in the Everglades,* Coral Gables: University of Miami Press, 1968, p.81

p. 53 Simmons, p. 22.

Chapter 5
p. 56 Carr, Archie, and the Editors of Time-Life Books, *The Everglades,* New York: Time-Life Books, 1973, p. 158

p. 64 Levin, Liquid Land, p. 210

p. 67 Douglas, Marjory Stoneman, with John Rothchild, *Voice of the River,* Sarasota: Pineapple Press, Inc., 1987, p. 231.

Chapter 6
p. 70 Jim Livingstone, Miami-Dade County municipal employee, telephone interview Sept. 29, 2005.

p. 79 Paul Gray, Okeechobee Science Coordinator, Lake Okeechobee Watershed Campaign Office, Telephone interview with author, May 2007.

p. 79 Douglas, *Voice of the River,* p. 231.

p. 80 Dr. Paul Grey, Science Coordinator, Lake Okeechobee Watershed Program, Audubon of Florida, telephone interview with author May 23, 2007.

p. 85 Marjory Stoneman Douglas (1890–1998), quoted in *Facing Florida's Environmental Future,* April 1990

Chapter 7

p. 87 Sam Bailey, Interview with the author, March 18, 2007

p. 89 Douglas, *Voice of the River,* p. 136

p. 89 Douglas, *Voice of the River,* p. 233

p. 94 Cook, Interview September 2005

Picture Credits

Photos were taken by author unless otherwise noted.

Page ii, middle and bottom: Courtesy of Jeanette Hobbs

Page iv, right: Courtesy of Jeanette Hobbs

Page viii, right: Courtesy of Sherrie Kreth

Page 3, drop cap: Photo by Bill Ake

Page 8: Courtesy of Jim Arendale

Page 14, top two and bottom left: Courtesy of Jeanette Hobbs

Page 18: Photo by Bill Ake

Page 23: James Newman, Florida Medical Entomology Laboratory C © 2003 University of Florida – IFAS

Page 30, bottom: Courtesy of Jeanette Hobbs

Page 32, top: Courtesy of National Park Service; bottom: Ginny Svoboda, courtesy of Homosassa State Wildlife Park

Page 34, top two, bottom left: Courtesy of Jeanette Hobbs; bottom right, David M. Dennis

Page 35: Courtesy of Jeanette Hobbs

Page 37: Courtesy of National Park Service

Page 38: Courtesy of Jeanette Hobbs

Page 40: Courtesy of Sherrie Kreth

Page 41: Courtesy of Jim Arendale

Page 44: Photo by Bill Ake

Page 46: Courtesy of the State Archives of Florida

Page 50: Courtesy of the State Archives of Florida

Page 51: Courtesy of the State Archives of Florida

Page 52, top: Courtesy of Sherrie Kreth

Page 55, drop cap: Courtesy of the Bonita Bay Group

Page 56: Courtesy of Sherrie Kreth

Page 64: Courtesy of Sherrie Kreth

Page 76: Courtesy of Jeanette Hobbs

Page 77, top: Conservancy of Southwest Florida

Page 80: Courtesy of Paul Gray

Page 82, all: Courtesy of the Bonita Bay Group

Page 88: Courtesy of the Bonita Bay Group

Page 89: Courtesy of the State Archives of Florida

Page 91: Courtesy of the National Park Service

Page 93, all: Arthur R. Marshall Foundation

Page 95: Courtesy of the National Park Service

Page 97: Virginia Svoboda, courtesy of Homosassa Springs Wildlife State Park

Page 99: Courtesy of Jeanette Hobbs

Back cover inset photos: Second photo by Bill Ake; Third photo courtesy of National Park Service; Bottom photo courtesy of Jeanette Hobbs

Glossary

Acre-foot—the volume of water that would cover one acre to a level of one foot deep. It equals 325,000 gallons of water.

Aquifer—a layer of porous rock, sand, or gravel through which groundwater flows, containing enough water to supply wells and springs.

Army Corps of Engineers—the engineering division of the U.S. Army. The Corps provides engineering services, including planning, designing, building, and operating water resources, and other civil works projects.

Berm—a raised bank at the edge of a road or along a canal.

Conifer—any tree that has thin leaves (needles) and produces cones. Many are evergreen, such as pines and spruces.

Custard apple—a wetland tree that bears a large fruit with black seeds and soft white flesh inside a green skin.

Crèche—a term adopted by behavioral biologists to describe a nursery of animals cared for by the female parent.

Deciduous—trees and shrubs that shed their leaves in the fall.

Degradation—in ecology, a decline in the quality of an ecosystem or habitat.

Duff—decaying leaves and branches covering a forest floor.

Ecology—the relationships and interactions between living organisms and their environment.

Ecosystem—a group of interdependent organisms and the environment that they live in and depend on.

Epiphyte—a plant that grows on top of or is supported by another plant but does not depend on it for nutrition. It obtains nutrients and moisture from the air and rain, and is sometimes called an air plant. Orchids and bromeliads are examples of this type of plant.

Estuary— partially enclosed coastal body of water. It is open to the ocean, and fresh water from inland is mixed with salt water from the sea. It is one of the most sensitive and ecologically important habitats on earth. Estuaries provide sanctuary for many species of waterfowl, store nutrients for larval and juvenile marine life, and serve as breeding grounds for many species of ocean fish.

Flowways—the natural flow patterns of water before humans began reshaping the land and redirecting the water.

Fossil fuels—carbon-containing fuel such as coal, peat, petroleum, and natural gas, derived from the decomposed remains of prehistoric plants and animals.

Fragmentation—the process of shattering or breaking up into fragments. When a habitat is broken into small scattered sections by development, animals have a hard time finding food, water, shelter, or a mate.

Habitat—the natural conditions and environment, for example, forest, desert, or wetlands, in which a plant or animal lives.

Hydrology—the study of earth's water including its properties, distribution, use, and circulation.

Indigenous—original or belonging to a place. Plants and animals that are native to a place.

Levee—an embankment to prevent flooding.

Limestone—sedimentary rock that consists chiefly of calcium carbonate. It is formed from the skeletons and shells of marine organisms.

Lock—a short section of a canal with gates at each end and machinery for raising and lowering water levels. Boats can be raised or lowered to the level of the next section of the waterway.

Microcosm—a miniature copy of something, expecially when it represents or stands for a larger whole.

Midden—in archaeology, a mound or area that contains domestic refuse such as food wastes, broken pottery, and other household items.

Oligotrophic—describes bodies of water that contain relatively low levels of nutrients, but are rich in dissolved oxygen.

Peat—a compacted deposit of partially decomposed organic debris, usually saturated with water. Because it is an anaerobic (meaning without oxygen) environment, it is a good medium for the preservation of archaeological remains.

Sedge—a wetland plant that resembles grass, but usually has a solid triangular stem.

Skiff—a small flatbottom boat of shallow draft that is usually propelled with oars, a sail, or a motor.

Skiffers—Gladesmen who made their living hunting and fishing from their skiffs.

SOFIA—South Florida Information Access is a service that provides information to support research, decision making, and resource management for the south Florida ecosystem restoration effort.

Solution hole—a depression in the Earth's surface caused by dissolving of underlying soil or stone composed primarily of calcium carbonate.

Subsidence—the sinking of land levels caused by natural shifts or human activity.

Subtropical—regions bordering on the tropical zone.

Succulent plant—a plant with thick fleshy leaves and stems that can store water.

Sustainable use—using natural resources without destroying the ecological balance of an ecosystem.

Transpiration—in botany, the loss of water vapor through a plant's surface, especially through minute surface pores.

Watershed—the land area that drains into a particular lake, river, or ocean.

Wetland—an area of land, such as a marsh or swamp, where the soil near the surface is saturated or covered with water for at least part of the year, especially one that forms a habitat for wildlife.

References

Books

Carr, Archie, and the Editors of Time-Life Books. *The Everglades*. Time-Life Books, 1973.
A detailed description of the ecosystem related in Carr's personal and enjoyable style.

Carter, W. Hodding. *Stolen Water: Saving the Everglades from Its Friends, Foes, and Florida*. New York: Atria Books, 2004.
A canoe trip through the Everglades spurs Carter to investigative research into Florida follies and politics. Carter's humor and keen perception make the book an enjoyable and instructive read.

Davis, Jack E., and Raymond Arsenault, Editors. *Paradise Lost? The Environmental History of Florida*. Gainesville, University Press of Florida, 2005.
A collection of essays describing the evolving environmental practices of Florida and the interaction between the environment and many social and cultural groups.

de Golla, Jack. *Everglades: The Story Behind the Scenery*. Las Vegas: KC Publications, 1978.
This book presents the story of the Everglades illustrated with beautiful photographs.

Douglas, Marjory Stoneman. *The Everglades: River of Grass*, 60th anniversary edition. Sarasota: Pineapple Press, Inc., 2007.
Originally published in 1947, Ms. Douglas's book helped draw public attention to the importance of the Everglades and the damage being done to the ecosystem. The 60th anniversary edition has an update by Michael Grunwald, author of *The Swamp: the Evergaldes, Florida, and the Politics of Paradise*.

Douglas, Marjory Stoneman, with John Rothchild. *Voice of the River*. Sarasota: Pineapple Press, Inc., 1987.
Rothchild edits more than 200 hours of taped interviews with Ms. Douglas to capture the wit, wisdom, and indomitable spirit of a remarkable lady.

Grunwald, Michael. *The Swamp: The Everglades, Florida, and the Politics of Paradise*. New York, Simon & Schuster, 2006.
Grunwald, winner of a Society of Environmental Journalist Award in 2003, focuses on the role Florida politics has played in the degradation and now the restoration attempt in the Everglades.

Levin, Ted. *Liquid Land: A Journey Through the Florida Everglades*. Athens: The University of Georgia Press, 2003.
Levin writes about the Everglades history, ecology, and politics, with emphasis on the conflicts inherent in the current restoration plan.

Pimm, Stuart L. *The World According to Pimm: A Scientist Audits the Earth*. New York: McGraw Hill, 2001.
Conservation biologist Pimm examines the huge detrimental impact humans have had on the planet.

Simmons, Glen, and Laura Ogden. *Gladesmen: Gator Hunters, Moonshiners, and Skiffers*. Gainesville: University Press of Florida, 1998.
The story of Glen Simmons' life in the Everglades in the early 1900s.

Storter, Rob, edited by Betty Savidge Briggs. *Crackers in the Glade: Life and Times in the Old Everglades*. Athens: University of Georgia Press, 2000.
Storter illustrates his tales of life in the old Everglades with his own drawings.

Tebeau, Charlton W. *Man in the Everglades: 2000 Years of Human History in the Everglades National Park*. Coral Gables: University of Miami Press, 1968.
Tebeau served as chair of the University of Miami's history department for 23 years of his 37-year tenure at the university. This exploration of human life in the Everglades is one of many important books he wrote on Florida history.

Internet sources

All About Birds, Cornell Lab of Ornithology, http://www.birds.cornell.edu/AllAboutBirds/BirdGuide/Great_Egret.html

Aquifer Storage and Recovery in the Comprehensive Everglades Restoration Plan, Executive Summary, National Academies Press, 2001, http://books.nap.edu/execsumm_pdf/10061.pdf

Arthur R. Marshall Foundation: Everglades Restoration, http://www.artmarshall.org/

Audubon of Florida, http://www.audubonofflorida.org/

Best Management Practices in the Everglades Agricultural Area: Controlling Particulate Phosphorus and Canal Sediments, O.A. Diaz, T.A. Lang, S.H. Daroub, and M. Chen, University of Florida IFAS Extension, August, 2005, http://edis.ifas.ufl.edu/pdffiles/SS/SS44800.pdf

"Biology of the Seaside Sparrow in the Everglades Region of Florida," William Post. http://www.sfrestore.org/sct/sparrow/3post2.doc

Everglades National Park Official Website, http://www.nps.gov/archive/ever/welcome2.htm

Florida Panther, Big Cat Rescue, http://www.bigcatrescue.org/florida_panther.htm

Fontaneda's Memoir. Jerry Wilkinson, editor, *Keys Historeum,* Historical Preservation Society of the Upper Keys. http://keyshistory.org/Fontenada.html

Lake Okeechobee Restoration, report prepared by Lake Okeechobee Science Coordinator Paul Gray, PhD, Everglades Science Coordinator Chris Farrell, and Everglades Policy Director Traci Romine, Audubon of Florida, http://www.audubon.org/states/fl/fl/PDFs/LakeOReport_1-07.pdf

Official Website of the Comprehensive Everglades Restoration Plan http://www.evergladesplan.org/index.aspx

Ramsar Bureau, Switzerland, "Wetland Values and Functions," http://www.ramsar.org/info/values_climate_e.pdf

Soil and Water Science, Everglades Agricultural Area Soil Subsidence and Land Use Projections. George H. Snyder, Distinguished Professor Emiritus. http://www.evergladesplan.org/pm/projects/project_docs/pdp_08_eaa_store/pdp_08_sub_land_use_report.pdf

Interviews

Rick Cook, Public Affairs Officer Everglades National Park, Telephone interview with author, September 12, 2005.

Paul Gray, Okeechobee Science Coordinator, Lake Okeechobee Watershed Campaign Office, Telephone interview with author, May 2007.

Jim Livingston, Telephone interview with author, September 29, 2005.

Larry Ogren, National Marine Fisheries, endangered species specialist, retired, Personal interviews with author from December 2004 through May 2007.

Jeff Schmid, Personal interviews with author, January 8, 2005 and March 24, 2007.

Periodicals

South Florida Environmental Report, Executive Summary, South Florida Water Management District, March 1, 2007.

Index

(Page numbers in **bold** indicate pictures.)

S

saltwater tolerant habitats, 10 (see *also* habitats)

Sanibel Island lighthouse, **49**

sawgrass, **57**
    and periphyton, 24
    and phosphorus 6, 8
    prairie, **2**

River of Grass, 24–26

Schmid, Dr. Jeffery, **21**, **98**

Schmid, Jill, **99**

seaside sparrow, 31, 35

Simmons, Glen, **50**

journal entries, 49–50, 53

on hard times, 42

slough, **5**, 6

snakebird (see anhinga)

snakes, 14
    mangrove, **14**

species count, 26

Storter, Rob, 48–49

strangler fig, **72** (see *also* epiphytes)

string lily, **58**

sugar
    burning field, **64**
    growing, 65
    processing plant, **62**
    statistics, 64

swamp, **9**
    cypress, **54**

T

Tamiami Trail, 51
    canal, **67**

environmental impact, 59
    tarpon, **56**

Tebeau, Charlton, 50

Ten Thousand Islands, 11, **13**

Tequesta, 44 (see *also* Indian tribes)

tortoise, 34
    gopher, **34**

tree islands, 8 (see *also* habitats)

tree snail, **76**

turtle, 34
    Kemp's ridley sea, **34**
    softshell, **34**

U

UNESCO, viii, 94

V

vulture, black, **20**

W

Water Resources Development Act of 2007, 70

water, 71
    sheet flow maps, 78

Wetland of International Importance, viii

wetland, 55–56

wood stork, **28**, 33, **35**

World Heritage Site, viii

Y

Yerian, Art, **97**

About the Author

Anne Ake has written five previous books for adult and young adult audiences, as well as numerous magazine articles on the arts, people, and nature. She has edited an arts magazine and published a children's magazine. Her photography has appeared in local and regional publications. She lives in north Florida.

Here are some other books from Pineapple Press on related topics. For a complete catalog, write to Pineapple Press, P.O. Box 3889, Sarasota, Florida 34230-3889, or call (800) 746-3275. Or visit our website at www.pineapplepress.com.

Everglades: River of Grass, 60th Anniversary Edition by Marjory Stoneman Douglas with an update by Michael Grunwald. Before 1947, when Marjory Stoneman Douglas named the Everglades a "river of grass," most people considered the area worthless. She brought the world's attention to the need to preserve the Everglades. In the Afterword, Michael Grunwald tells us what has happened to them since then. (hb)

Priceless Florida by Ellie Whitney, D. Bruce Means, and Anne Rudloe. An extensive guide (432 pages, 800 color photos) to the incomparable ecological riches of this unique region, presented in a way that will appeal to young and old, laypersons and scientists. Complete with maps, charts, species lists. (hb, pb)

The Florida Water Story by Peggy Sias Lantz and Wendy A. Hale. Illustrated by Jean Barnes. Introduces young readers to Florida's water systems and describes and illustrates many of the plants and animals that depend on these watery habitats. (hb)

The Young Naturalist's Guide to Florida, 2nd Edition, by Peggy Sias Lantz and Wendy A. Hale. Newly updated. Complete with a glossary, this enticing book shows you where and how to look for Florida's most interesting natural features and creatures. Take it along on your next walk in the woods. (pb)

Drawing Florida's Wildlife by Frank Lohan. The clearest, easiest method yet for learning to draw Florida's birds, reptiles, amphibians, and mammals. (pb)

The Gopher Tortoise by Patricia Sawyer Ashton and Ray E. Ashton Jr. Color photos and easy text make clear the behavior and daily life of the gopher tortoise. Find out how scientists study these unique animals and try to protect them from human encroachment on their habitat. (hb, pb)

Dinosaurs of the South by Judy Cutchins and Ginny Johnston. Dinosaurs lived in the southeastern United States. Loaded with full-color fossil photos as well as art to show what dinos might have looked like. (hb)

Ice Age Giants of the South by Judy Cutchins and Ginny Johnston. Learn about the huge animals and reptiles that lived here during the Ice Age. Meet saber-toothed cats, dire wolves, mammoths, giant sloths, and more. (hb)

Giant Predators of the Ancient Seas by Judy Cutchins and Ginny Johnston. Meet the giant creatures that prowled the waters of prehistory. (hb)

Those Amazing Alligators by Kathy Feeney. Illustrated by Steve Weaver, photographs by David M. Dennis. Alligators are amazing animals, as you'll see in this book. Discover the differences between alligators and crocodiles; learn what alligators eat, how they communicate, and much more. (hb, pb)

Those Terrific Turtles by Sarah Cussen. Illustrated by Steve Weaver, photographs by David M. Dennis. You'll learn the difference between a turtle and a tortoise, and find out why they have shells. Meet baby turtles and some very, very old ones, and even explore a pond. (hb, pb)